WHY BLOCKCHAIN

Where Privacy & Transparency Coexist

Written By
Harman Puri

Copyright © Harmanpreet Singh Puri 2023
All Rights Reserved.

ISBN 979-8-89067-993-2

This book has been published with all efforts taken to make the material error-free after the consent of the author. However, the author and the publisher do not assume and hereby disclaim any liability to any party for any loss, damage, or disruption caused by errors or omissions, whether such errors or omissions result from negligence, accident, or any other cause.

While every effort has been made to avoid any mistake or omission, this publication is being sold on the condition and understanding that neither the author nor the publishers or printers would be liable in any manner to any person by reason of any mistake or omission in this publication or for any action taken or omitted to be taken or advice rendered or accepted on the basis of this work. For any defect in printing or binding the publishers will be liable only to replace the defective copy by another copy of this work then available.

CONTENTS

FOREWORD

Harman Puri has done a wonderful job with the illustrative narrative on blockchain and decentralization giving rise to multifarious concepts in the eight chapters of the book, "WHY BLOCKCHAIN". A developer can be a great illustrator and teacher generally speaking and that is how the growth of Harman happened. It has become really productive with this book in our hand.

In the digital chronicles of our time, few innovations have spurred as much excitement, skepticism, and profound shifts as blockchain and the broader movement towards decentralization. What began as the underlying technology for a novel digital currency in 2008 has since blossomed into a revolutionary paradigm that promises to redefine the very fabric of our global systems.

The idea of a decentralized system — where power and control are distributed among its participants rather than being concentrated in a single central authority — is not new. Historically, we have seen decentralized structures in various societal frameworks. However, it is the technological interpretation and application of this idea, largely through blockchain, that has the potential to bring about unprecedented transparency, resilience, and empowerment.

In "WHY BLOCKCHAIN" we embark on a journey that delves deep into the multifaceted world of decentralized technology. From its nascent days with the invention of Bitcoin to the sprawling ecosystem of tokens, smart contracts, decentralized applications, and beyond, this book endeavors to illuminate the intricacies of blockchain technology for both the novice and the seasoned expert.

But this journey isn't limited to mere technology. We surf thru the pages and try to gauge how will blockchain redefine institutions and systems? What implications does blockchain hold for supply chain, healthcare, ZKP, and asset tokenization?

The myriad possibilities of blockchain and decentralization bring to mind the heady days of the early internet. Just as the internet democratized information, the blockchain has the potential to democratize trust, ownership, and collaboration.

However, with great potential comes equally formidable challenges.

Scalability, volatility, energy consumption, regulation, and adoption barriers are all hurdles that this nascent industry must overcome. Yet, as history has shown, with challenges come innovations and solutions that often surpass our wildest expectations.

As you delve into these pages, it is my hope that you& will emerge with a well- rounded understanding, not just of technology but also of its broader implications and transformative power. Whether you are a developer, entrepreneur, student, policymaker, or just a curious mind, this book will serve as both a guide and a source of inspiration. Embrace the era of decentralization, for in it lies the promise of a future that is more transparent, equitable, and, ultimately, empowering for all. I have no qualms in stating that EST FAB shall take this book as a primary resource book on Blockchain. It is simple, subtle, illustrative and easily comprehensible.

Welcome to the journey of the blockchain world created and sketched by Harman. I wish him a real transformative success through changing technologies.

Dr. Sindhu
Chairman & Founder
FORBES Council Member
EST GLOBAL INC.
Cambridge Innovation Center
One Broadway, 14th floor,
Cambridge, MA 02142 USA
Email: sindhu@estglobalinc.com
http://linkedin.com/in/sindhu-bhaskar-55a84568
Web: www.estglobalinc.com
www.estfab.com/www.esticg.com/www.estagrx.com

PROLOGUE

From personal photographs and social media posts to financial records and healthcare information, data is omnipresent. As the digital world continues to expand, so does the significance of how this data is stored, transferred, and secured. The need for a technology that can protect and streamline the exchange of vast amounts of data has never been more crucial.

Enter Blockchain, a groundbreaking technology that promises to revolutionize the way we interact with data. This book aims to provide students with an accessible and comprehensive guide to the world of Blockchain. Whether a complete novice or somewhat familiar with the concept, readers will find clear explanations, real-world examples, and insights that demystify this transformative technology.

Together, we will explore the foundations, applications, and future possibilities of Blockchain, opening doors to innovation and a more secure digital landscape.

Blockchain is a fundamental technology acting as the base for the next industrial revolution.

Chapter 1

THE IOS STATEMENT

Every click, every transaction, and every digital interaction generates gigabytes and terabytes of data. This data has become the lifeblood of an increasingly connected society. In fact, it is often said that data is the new oil, the new currency, the new gold rush. In this fervor for data, however, there are pressing issues that continue to be obstacles to the smooth functioning of a data-driven world.

When individuals encounter statements such as:

- A social media platform is stealing user data.
- A company is using data to manipulate users into buying.
- Users are receiving credit card calls, indicating that data may have been leaked.

These expressions lead to a common reaction: attributing blame to multinational corporations, portraying them as malicious, exploitative, and manipulative, seemingly holding a monopoly over information.

However, in exploring the intricacies of the modern world, it is crucial to reassess these assumptions.

The pertinent questions arise:

- Why do these corporations have access to personal data in the first place?
- Can users leverage these innovative platforms without constant anxiety over data privacy?
- Is there another way to store data with high security measures?

As we delve deeper into the matrix of data, three terms continuously emerge as pillars of what we seek from our data systems. These terms form the bedrock of our digital interactions - **Integrity, Ownership, and Security.**

Collectively, we refer to these as the **IOS statement**, a trinity of principles essential to maintaining the efficacy of our data landscape. And no, this IOS has nothing to do with the iPhones, but it is much more significant than that.

Defining the IOS statement

Integrity

Integrity of data refers to the accuracy and consistency of data throughout its entire lifecycle i.e. when it is created, shared, stored, accessed, modified, or deleted. Integrity is concerned with ensuring that the data generated by a user remains unchanged unless altered by an authorized entity. If a bank's ledger displays inconsistent balances at different times without any documented transactions, it constitutes a violation of data integrity. Thus, the assurance that data remains undisturbed and uncorrupted is a fundamental requirement.

Ownership

Within the vast expanse of the internet, establishing the ownership of a piece of data can be a complex task. Ownership is not only concerned with who created the data but also who may use it, alter it, or benefit from it. In a contemporary world where data can be copied, changed, and redistributed with just a few clicks, determining data ownership has emerged as a pressing concern. A simple example might be a photograph taken by a user being used without consent or attribution - an infringement of data ownership.

Security

Given the increasing prevalence of cyber-attacks, data breaches, and hacking incidents, the security of data has become paramount. Security pertains to the safeguarding of data against unauthorized access, use, disclosure, disruption, or destruction. The unauthorized access of personal data by an unknown entity not only violates privacy but also raises questions regarding the effectiveness of data security protocols.

These three pillars, Integrity, Ownership, and Security, comprise the IOS statement. IOS represents issues that are foundational to digital interactions and challenges that current data systems continue to wrestle with.

Generally, separate actions or measures are required to individually address these critical factors such as installing firewalls for security, maintaining records for ownership, and creating audit trail for integrity.

But what if there was a technology that could collectively address these issues? A tool that could fortify these pillars, and bring about a revolution in the way we handle data.

This is where Blockchain comes in.

> *The old question 'Is it in the database?' will be replaced by 'Is it on the blockchain?'*
>
> *- William Mougayar*

Blockchain, at its core, is a new kind of database system that brings a radical shift to the conventional methods of handling data, a shift that provides solutions to the IOS statement. By leveraging decentralization, Blockchain ensures that data is not stored in one central point, reducing the risk of data tampering and increasing security. By creating a transparent ledger of data, it enforces integrity and ownership, making sure every change is tracked and attributed to a specific entity.

Blockchain doesn't just promise solutions, it provides a path to redefining the foundation of our digital interactions.

But why is Blockchain so crucial to the IOS statement? Why should society invest time, effort, and resources in understanding this technology?

The reason is simple.

Data is the beating heart of society, and the IOS statement serves as its pulse. To ensure that the heart remains healthy, and the pulse remains steady, there is a necessity for a system that is robust, secure, and trustworthy. That is precisely what Blockchain aims to provide.

Let us examine the IOS statement in further detail by considering one prominent example for each characteristic:

Data Integrity: The Case of ChatGPT

Imagine for a moment that a user is interacting with ChatGPT, the sophisticated AI model developed by OpenAI. This AI model has been trained on a vast dataset comprising diverse types of content from the Internet. It utilizes that training to provide information and engage in intelligent conversations. Users pose questions to it, trusting in its capabilities to provide accurate and reliable answers.

But what if the data used to train this AI had been compromised?

Consider, for example, a situation where someone manipulated the data in ChatGPT's training set, introducing a significant number of false historical events, skewed scientific facts, or misleading news stories. Since ChatGPT learns and generates responses based on this data, the manipulated input would lead to the AI disseminating incorrect, potentially harmful information.

A person querying ChatGPT about a historical event might receive a fabricated account. A student seeking explanations for a scientific concept could be misled with incorrect theories. Even more concerning, a user seeking advice on health or legal matters might be provided with dangerous suggestions that could lead to severe repercussions.

This scenario emphasizes the critical importance of data integrity. It is not merely about the accuracy of information; it affects trust, decision-making, and in some instances, can have extensive impacts on individual lives and society as a whole.

Enter Blockchain Technology

In a scenario where the training data for ChatGPT is stored and managed using blockchain technology, such manipulation could be avoided. Blockchain's immutable nature means that once data is added to the blockchain, it cannot be altered without the consensus of the network. This ensures that the data used to train AI models like ChatGPT remains trustworthy, maintaining the integrity of the information provided.

Moreover, each block in a blockchain contains a cryptographic hash of the previous block, creating a linked chain of data blocks (explained further in Chapter 2). This means that even if someone attempts to tamper with a block of data, the entire network would be alerted, as it would break the link with the previous block and disrupt the chain. This additional layer of security safeguards the training data against unauthorized alterations, reinforcing the integrity of the AI responses.

In essence, by utilizing blockchain technology, the training data of AI models like ChatGPT could be secured against unauthorized modifications, ensuring that the AI's output remains reliable and accurate. The protection of data integrity through blockchain is not solely about maintaining the quality of AI conversations; it encompasses preserving trust, preventing misinformation, and ultimately, forging a more reliable digital future.

The same concept applies to various interactions in daily life, such as:

- Consuming news
- Securing Medical Records
- Processing Insurance claims
- Protecting Identity
- Ensuring Food Safety
- Securing IoT Devices
- Authenticating Academic Credentials
- Facilitating Fair Trade
- Preventing Election Fraud
- Safeguarding Creative Works

And many more

Potentially, any system where data is created or consumed needs to ensure the integrity of that data.

Data Ownership: Instagram and Memes

In an era where content creation has become a livelihood for many, the boundaries of ownership have blurred. Data ownership is a critical issue, especially on platforms such as Instagram, where creativity thrives and user-generated content forms the backbone of the platform.

Consider the following scenario to illustrate this point:

- Imagine a user, Anjali, who is an avid participant on Instagram. One day, Anjali creates a meme, an amusing and perceptive commentary on a current event, and posts it on an account with a modest following. Unfortunately, the meme doesn't gain much traction
- A few days later, Anjali notices something startling. An Instagram influencer, boasting a following of 20 million users, posts the exact same meme — Anjali's meme. The influencer fails to give credit, and the post becomes viral, receiving thousands of likes, shares, and comments.
- This influencer, who monetizes the Instagram account through sponsorship arrangements, indirectly profits from Anjali's creation. They reap the benefits of Anjali's creativity, while the original creator gains nothing.
- Attempts to claim ownership may prove challenging and protracted, as establishing oneself as the original creator may not be straightforward.
- What if there were a technology that could unquestionably identify Anjali as the original creator of the meme? A system that could guarantee that, no matter where the meme ended up, it would always be linked back to Anjali, the original creator?

Enter Blockchain Technology.

Blockchain, a decentralized and immutable ledger system, is a perfect a solution to this issue of data ownership. When a user creates a piece of content - a meme in this case - it gets uploaded onto a blockchain platform designed for content creators. Once the meme is added to the blockchain, it creates a 'block' - a permanent, unalterable record that verifies the user as the original creator at a specific date and time. This block, containing the ownership information, is then added to a chain of similar blocks - hence the term, blockchain.

When the influencer reposts the meme, blockchain technology can trace the meme's origins back to the user's original post. Therefore, the blockchain record serves as an irrefutable proof of data ownership. This ownership record is public, transparent, and secure from tampering due to the decentralized and immutable nature of blockchain technology.

Moreover, blockchain can also facilitate fair compensation for the creation. Through smart contracts - self-executing contracts with the terms directly written into the code - user could automatically receive payment or recognition every time their meme is used or reposted. This ensures that the user, as the original content creator, receives their deserved credit and compensation.

In a world where data has become a valuable commodity, blockchain can help uphold the rights of individual content creators. By ensuring data ownership and facilitating fair compensation, blockchain not only encourages creativity but also fosters trust and transparency in the digital content ecosystem.

This chapter's scenario is a simple illustration of the potential of blockchain technology to redefine the concept of data ownership. But the implications are far-reaching, extending beyond memes on Instagram to all forms of digital content and intellectual property.

As we explore further in this book, we will delve deeper into the profound impact blockchain can have on our digital lives.

Data Security: Your Search History

Every user's online activities, no matter how trivial, are constantly monitored, collected, and analyzed. Personal data from these online activities is harvested by companies, that use this information to tailor advertisements, influence buying habits, and drive profits. However, this often happens without a user's explicit knowledge or consent, leading to concerns about data privacy and security.

Consider this: you have been casually browsing for shoes online, or maybe you have mentioned needing a new pair of shoes during a call through your smartphone. Suddenly, you notice that every other advertisement on your social media feeds is for shoes. They're not just any shoes, but shoes that match your style, your preferred price range, even the specific occasions for which you might need them.

But how is this ad by a random company so personalized? The answer is data.

Third-party data companies aggregate information about your online behavior, including your search history, shopping habits, and even your conversations. They couple this with your personal data such as your age, location, credit score, and occupation to create a detailed profile of you as a consumer.

This profile becomes the base for the advertisements you see. Companies pay hefty sums for this information so they can target you with highly specific ads for products you're likely to buy. The shoes you casually mentioned become an omnipresent suggestion, subtly nudging you towards a purchase.

While this personalization can sometimes be convenient, it raises serious questions about data security and privacy. Your personal data is being collected, shared, and used without your explicit consent. This level of surveillance can feel intrusive and can lead to misuse of data, potential identity theft, and other security risks.

Enter Blockchain Technology

Blockchain's decentralization and encryption capabilities could give control of personal data back to the user. Instead of personal data being stored on a centralized server, susceptible to breaches and unauthorized access, it would be distributed across a blockchain network. This would make unauthorized access extremely difficult, if not impossible.

Moreover, with blockchain, you could choose when and how your data is shared. For instance, instead of third-party companies monitoring your every move online, you could choose to share specific data in exchange for personalized advertisements. You might consent to sharing your shoe size and preferred styles but opt to keep your location or credit score private.

Blockchain could also authenticate how your data is used through smart contracts. These contracts would enforce the agreed-upon terms of data usage, ensuring companies only use your data in ways you've approved.

Through this approach, blockchain can bring about a shift in the power dynamics of the digital landscape, putting users back in control of their personal data. This not only enhances data security but also respects user privacy, allowing for personalized experiences without the fear of intrusive surveillance or data misuse.

How Blockchain Can Help Monetize Data

When a person thinks about monetizing assets, they usually think about physical items or services that can be offered. However, in the digital age, one of the most valuable assets one can possess is **data**. Every interaction, every click, every digital footprint is a valuable piece of information, not just for a user but also for businesses, researchers, and governments.

The question remains, "can this data be monetised?" And more importantly, can it be done securely, while maintaining ownership and integrity of the data?

Enter Blockchain Technology

Let's consider an example that brings together all the aspects we have been discussing: health records.

Healthcare data is a treasure trove of information, not just for doctors and hospitals, but also for pharmaceutical companies, researchers, insurance providers, and even technology firms developing health apps. Traditionally, hospitals might share health records of their patients with a research facility for a study, often without the knowledge or explicit consent of the patients.

Now, imagine if the patients could take control of this process. With blockchain technology, they can.

In a blockchain-based healthcare data system, the health records would be stored in a secure, encrypted block. The patient would hold the 'key' or access rights to this block. This means that any entity wanting to access the health record data would have to request the permission of the patient. **This enables security of the data.**

With the aid of smart contracts, even the terms of data access can be set and enforced. Maybe a patient agrees to share their data with a local university for a study, but not with a pharmaceutical company. Or perhaps another patient wants to support cancer research, so they give their consent to researchers doing cancer studies, but not in any other types of research. **This enables Ownership of the data.**

Beyond maintaining control of the data, blockchain can also allow to monetize it. Instead of hospitals or other intermediaries benefitting from the use of the health record data, patients could receive compensation directly. If a research institution finds a particular health record valuable for their study, they could pay the patient directly to access that data.

Furthermore, the trustless nature of this system could actually encourage more institutions to access data directly from individuals because the blockchain guarantees the integrity of that data. The information cannot be tampered with or altered, meaning researchers can trust its authenticity and completeness. On the other hand, it will encourage more people to come forward and provide authentic data for research, incentivization being an added motivation. **This enables integrity of data.**

Therefore, the scenario of monetizing health data is a testament to the three fundamental aspects we've discussed:

Data integrity is maintained. As soon as the health record data is put on the blockchain, it can't be changed or tampered with, not even by the patient themselves since Blockchain is append only.

Data ownership is clear. Patients own their health data, and they decide who gets access to it through cryptographic keys.

Data security is enforced. The data is encrypted and stored on a decentralized network, protecting it from breaches, both internal and external.

The blockchain puts the user back in control of their data - whether they choose to keep it private or monetize it. It offers an innovative way to approach data, turning it from something often exploited into a valuable asset that can be controlled and benefitted from. As we move further into the digital age, technologies like blockchain will help shape a fair, secure, and user-centric digital ecosystem.

Chapter 2

WHAT IS BLOCKCHAIN

Blockchain is a decentralised and distributed ledger containing digital transactions that are cryptographically linked and chronologically added through the consensus protocol.

While the general definition of Blockchain seems rather overwhelming, the following sections will break it down to the simplest possible explanation.

This chapter is divided into two parts: Part one explains the individual technologies that form the Blockchain network, part two explains how exactly a Blockchain operates and helps us understand Blockchain through real life example.

Part 1

Blockchain is a tool to democratize digital interactions.

Beyond the commonly used description of Blockchain as merely a distributed ledger, we recognize its true nature and potential. Blockchain is a technology, a method, or sometimes even a concept that enables the creation of a digital network with distinct characteristics. These characteristics are unattainable with current systems and therefore set Blockchain apart, highlighting its unique capabilities. While there can be multiple properties defining the necessity of Blockchain, mentioned below are the 5 most commonly considered factors for integrating Blockchain in a system.

1. Unbiased
2. Secure
3. Transparent
4. Immutable
5. Decentralized

Defining the Blocks of Blockchain

Think of Blockchain as a collection of multiple concepts that come together to form an unbreakable system.

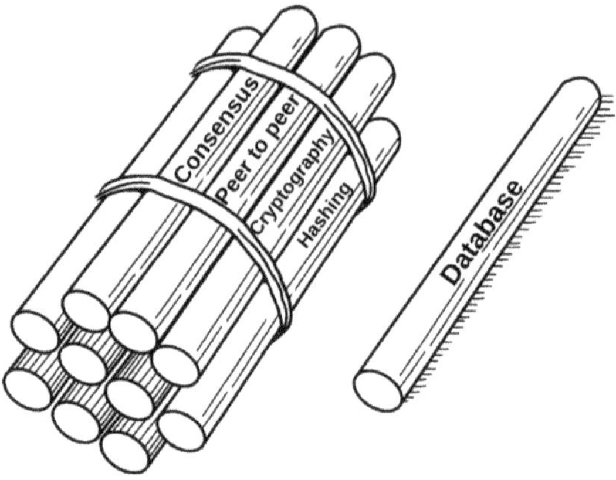

The popular childhood story of how "one single stick can be broken but if multiple sticks are bundled together, they cannot be broken" is a perfect example.

Blockchain is a similar bundle of different concepts that cannot be broken.

Individually, these concepts have existed for a long time and while they have been instrumental in many applications, Blockchain is undeniably the most significant technology they have produced by coming together.

Let us evaluate all of these concepts by defining three key aspects:

What, Why, and How

In the following section, we establish what these concepts are, why they came into being, and how they are being used.

Note: we are not going to discuss these technologies in detail since our main objective is to understand the core concept of Blockchain.

1. Cryptography

- **What:** Cryptography is a method of protecting information by transforming it into an unreadable format. It uses algorithms to encrypt and decrypt data, thus ensuring secure communication.
- **Why:** Cryptography is crucial for secure communication in the digital world, protecting information from unauthorized access or alteration. It is used extensively in securing network communications, financial transactions, and personal data.
- **How:** Cryptography works by using encryption algorithms and cryptographic keys. Data is encrypted using a specific key, turning it into ciphertext. The same key (symmetric encryption) or a different but mathematically related key (asymmetric encryption) is then used to decrypt the data, turning it back into its original form.

2. Hashing

- **What:** Hashing is a method of converting any size of data into a fixed length of output, often referred to as a hash value or hash code. The original data always produces the same fixed length of output but the output can never be reverse engineered to get back the input.
- **Why:** Hashing is commonly used for data retrieval, password storage, data integrity checks, and in blockchain technology. It improves data retrieval speed in databases and ensures data integrity in communications. Most importantly, hashing is creatively used to maintain data integrity by minimizing storage requirements. This is a key concept that we will discuss in a separate chapter.
- **How:** Hashing works by taking an input (or 'message') and returning a fixed-size string of characters and numbers. The output is unique to each unique input. Any small change in the input will produce such drastic changes in output that the new hash value appears uncorrelated with the old hash value.

3. Peer-to-peer network

- **What:** A peer-to-peer (P2P) network is a decentralized network where each node, a computer system or 'peer', shares a part of its resources directly with other nodes without the need for a central server.
- **Why:** P2P networks are used for sharing content like audio, video, data, or anything in digital format. They're also used in blockchain networks, telecommunications, and streaming media. They offer increased redundancy, improved load distribution, and resistance to censorship in addition to demonopolizing the network from central authorities.
- **How:** In a P2P network, each node acts as both a client and a server, offering a portion of its resources, such as processing power, disk storage, or network bandwidth, directly to other nodes.

4. Consensus algorithms

- **What**: Consensus algorithms are protocols used in distributed systems (like blockchain) to achieve agreement on a single data value among distributed processes or systems. In other words, the Consensus algorithm is a way to achieve mutual agreement between non-trusting anonymous parties.
- **Why**: They are crucial for ensuring reliability, synchronicity, and fault tolerance in distributed systems or networks. They're used in various applications, from distributed databases to blockchain networks. We will be discussing consensus algorithms in detail in the third chapter since Consensus is one of the most important concepts in blockchain technology.
- **How**: Consensus algorithms like Proof-of-Work, Proof-of-Stake, and several others, function by setting rules and conditions that nodes in the network must comply with to reach an agreement, mutually.

5. Distributed computing

- **What**: Distributed computing involves multiple computers in a network working together to solve a computational problem.

- **Why**: Distributed computing systems are used when a computational task is too significant or complex to be handled by a single machine. They also offer redundancy and can ensure that the system continues to operate even if individual machines fail.
- **How**: In a distributed system, the computational task is divided into smaller tasks, which are distributed among the nodes in the network. Each node solves its portion of the problem, and the results are combined to form the final solution.

6. Database

- **What**: A database is an organized collection of data that can be easily accessed, managed, and updated.
- **Why**: Databases are essential for storing and managing data efficiently. They are used in a wide range of applications, from small-scale applications like websites to large-scale applications like social networks and banking systems.
- **How**: Data in a database is typically structured in rows, columns, and tables to efficiently manage, insert, update, and delete data. Databases use a language called SQL (Structured Query Language) for these operations. There are also non-relational databases, often referred to as NoSQL databases, that use different models for data storage and retrieval.

Now that we are familiar with the necessary concepts, let us utilise this knowledge and understand a step by step approach to how a Blockchain actually works.

In the following section, we will go through 6 steps that defined the process of how data is added into a Blockchain. In the subsequent section, we will be taking a real-life example to understand these steps in further detail.

Part 2

The Blockchain Process

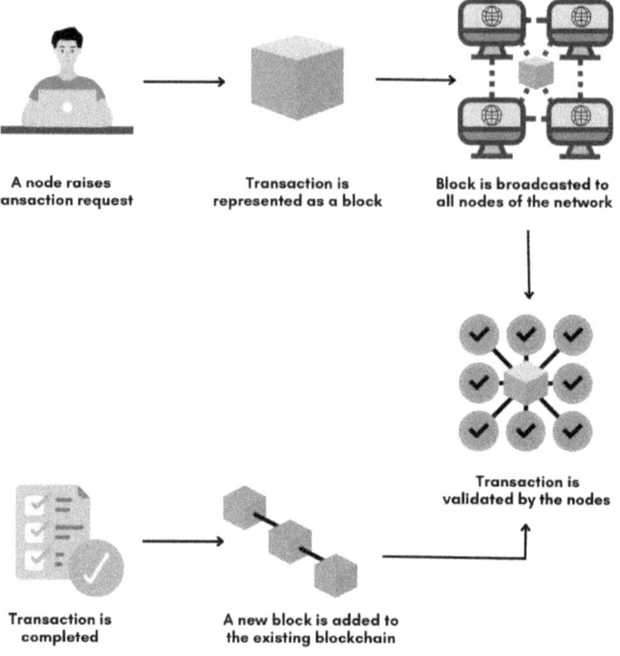

Step 1: Transaction Creation

A user initiates a transaction, such as sending digital currency to another user. This transaction includes the public key of the recipient (akin to their unique address), the amount being sent, and the sender's digital signature, created using their private key. This digital signature, a product of cryptography, is the sender's way of securely authorizing the transaction.

Step 2: Transaction Verification

Before the transaction can be added to the blockchain, it must be verified. This is where the peer-to-peer network comes in. The network's nodes (computers participating in the blockchain by maintaining the ledger), check the transaction details, ensuring the sender has enough balance for the transaction and that the digital signature matches the sender's public key along with several other factors required for verification. This system ensures the authenticity and validity of the transaction.

Step 3: Block Formation

Once the transaction is verified, it's combined with other verified transactions into a 'block.' This block contains data of the transactions, a timestamp and a reference to the hash of the previous block in the chain. Hashing ensures that any change in the transaction data is quickly noticeable as it drastically alters the resulting hash.

Step 4: Block Addition

Next, the Consensus algorithms ensures that the new data entry in the Blockchain complies with its predefined rules. In the case of Bitcoin's blockchain, the Proof-of-Work consensus algorithm is used. This step secures the block's position in the chain, and the linked list nature of the blockchain ensures the immutability of previous blocks.

Step 5: Block distribution

After a block is added to the chain, the updated version of the blockchain is propagated across the network, with each node updating their copy. This distributed computing aspect ensures redundancy and the decentralized nature of the blockchain, with each node storing a copy of the entire blockchain.

Step 6: Confirmation of Transaction

Finally, the transaction is confirmed and considered complete once it's part of a block in the chain. The receiver, now certain of the transaction's immutability, can consider the transaction successful.

This step-by-step process exemplifies how the different technologies underpinning blockchain - cryptography, hashing, peer-to-peer networks, consensus algorithms, and distributed computing - play their parts in storing data securely and transparently on the blockchain.

Let us go through an example to understand the inner workings of the Blockchain in more detail.

The Perfect Example

Imagine you are sitting in an auditorium.

There are 100 other people sitting in the same auditorium but you don't know anyone neither does anyone knows each other.

100 anonymous people in one room.

Now, you stand up and say, "I want a loan of 10 Lakh and I am ready to pay a 5% interest rate for a tenure of 2 months."

Some anonymous person from the crowd stands up and says, "I can give you that required amount but what collateral are you going to keep as security"

You have a Fixed Deposit of 20 Lakh that you don't want to break since you will get interest on it after 3 years. So, you put your FD as collateral to get the loan.

Without any central authority, how will you resolve possible conflicts or trust this anonymous person?

Here are some possible challenges:

What if,

- The lender retrieves the FD before 2 months to get money back fast
- The borrower keeps extending the deadline
- The borrower or lender try to cheat by changing the interest rate or tenure

There are multiple possible situations that can arise which is the whole reason we have a central authority in the first place.

However, by this time, we have come to realize that the pros and cons of having a central authority should be considered equally.

While central authorities do help in keeping harmony and standardization, they enjoy a power which is dangerous. Time and again, the world has faced consequences when one central authority abuses their powers or becomes a monopoly.

The 2008 economic crisis, the great depression, etc. Therefore, we want to create a system where this harmony and standardization can be maintained without a central authority.

In this case, the following steps will be taken to complete the transaction.

You, along with the lender, write down your transaction on a piece of paper.

Let's assume your name is John and the Lender is Carl.

The paper says:

"John has borrowed 10 Lakh from Carl at an interest of 5% for a tenure of 2 months. John has put his Fixed Deposit of 20 Lakh as a collateral and in case John is not able to return the money on time, he will break his Fixed Deposit and give the money back to Carl."

However, this is just a piece of paper, anyone can produce a copy or change it.

Let's make it more secure by *distributing.*

John and Carl ask all the other 98 anonymous people in the room to write down the transaction details on their notebooks.

The day ends, everyone goes back home.

Now, Since John had a Fixed Deposit of 20 Lakh, Carl thinks:

> "If only I could change the transaction record, I can cheat John and take all of his 20 Lakh by saying that he borrowed 20 Lakh from me in the first place instead of the original 10 Lakh."

The problem now will be, Carl can change his record, and maybe even John's record, but John can verify from any one of the 98 people in the room who have written the same record on their notebooks and taken it back home.

Carl does not know the identity of any of those people so he has to firstly find who all were in the room, then locate their homes, and then go to each of their homes to change their records.

In a similar way, all the 98 people do transactions for their respective needs. Some borrow, some lend, but no one knows each other.

The only thing they have in common is a notebook that contains the transactional details of all the people.

Therefore, all they have is a ***shared ledger*** of transactions.

> *This forms the decentralized ledger component of the Blockchain which replaces the role of a central authority to maintain a record of transactions for enforcing trust.*

In a similar way to how we established the importance of having a shared ledger, we will now discuss the possible challenges in this situation and what steps we can take to overcome them.

With each challenge, we will consider one of the previous 5 components we discussed and how those components can help solve the proposed challenge.

Challenge 1

While sharing transactional data, there are two critical issues.

1. The transactional data is so long for each transaction that notebooks of individual people keeps getting filled and they need new notebooks.

2. By sharing the identity and other details of people performing a transaction, the crowd no more stays anonymous.

We solve this through **hashing.**

Both John and Carl, put their transactional detail in a hashing algorithm which gives them a unique output of fixed length.

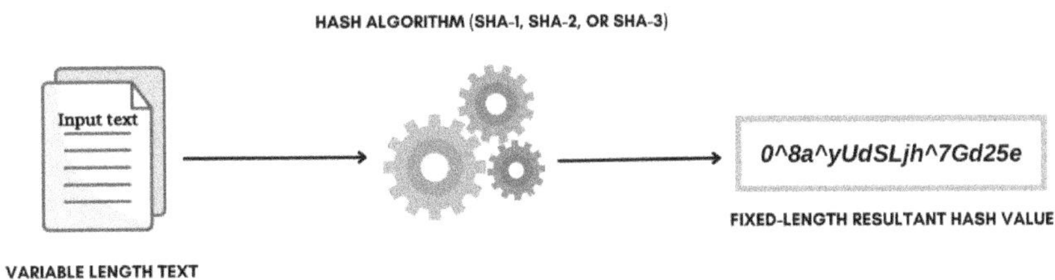

Now, instead of sharing their transactional data, they are sharing the hash of their data with all 98 people.

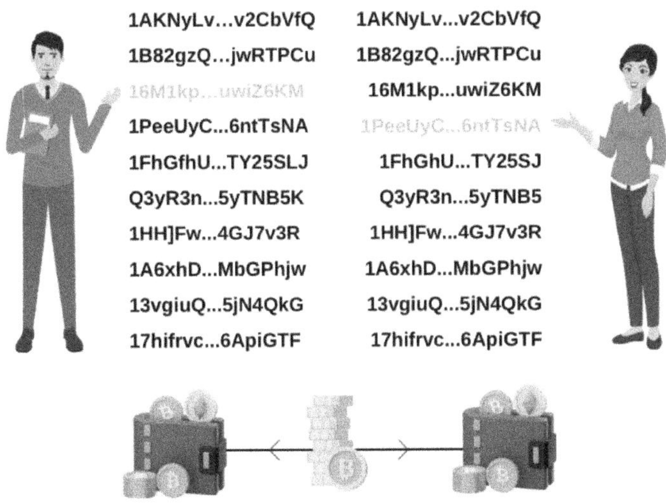

Even a small full stop, a change in case, any minor change in the original data will produce a drastically changed hash.

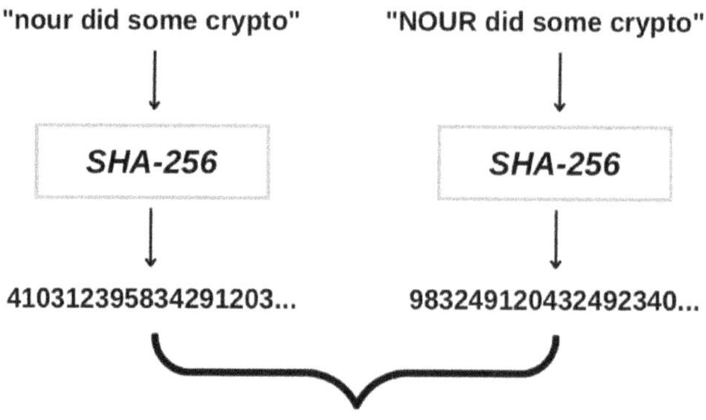

In case of conflict, either of the parties can just go to any of the 98 people and match the hash in their record with the hash of the data that resides with John or Carl. Whichever hash matches, the corresponding data will be considered for conflict resolution.

Therefore, if the data with John does not match the data with Carl, both John and Carl will convert their data into a hash and match it with the record of the crowd. A successful match will reveal who is honest and who is cheating, without ever revealing their true data.

Challenge 2

What if Carl has a highly intelligent team who is good at finding all those anonymous people and then changing the hash on their records so that Carl can manipulate the system?

*To solve this, we create a **cryptographic link** between the records.*

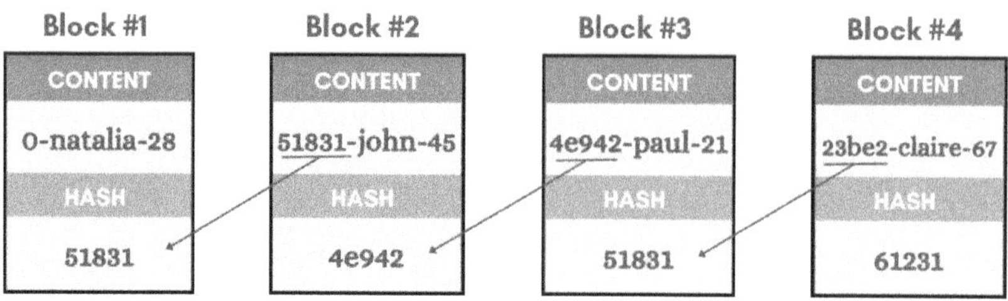

When John and Carl do a transaction and share its hash with 98 people, we make a small addition.

In addition to the data of the transaction, we add the hash of a previous transaction that has been done by 2 or more of those 98 anonymous people.

Therefore,

Data of transaction + the hash of the previous transaction is combined together to form a new hash.

Similarly, any new transaction from those 98 people will be combined with the hash of John and Carl's transaction.

Remember, even a small change in data will produce a drastically changed hash which will never match the original data hash.

To manipulate the system now, Carl does not just need to change the hash on the distributed record but he has to change all the transactions following his transaction.

Why?

Because a change in his transaction will change the hash of the transaction.

This hash is used in the next transaction to calculate a new hash which now changes too, and same with the next transaction and the next and the next.

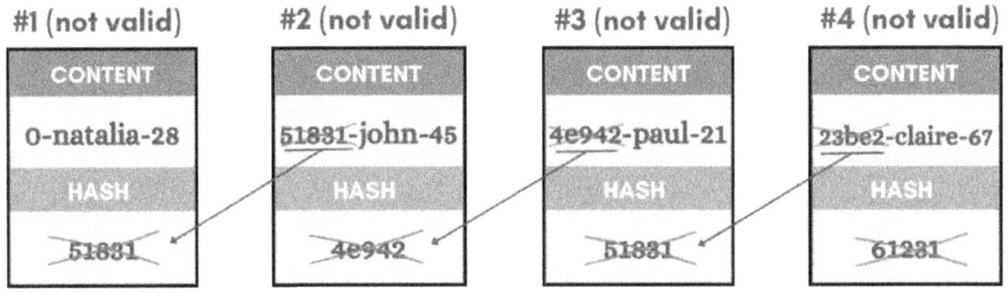

In simpler terms, this cryptographic link between transactions is why it is called a Blockchain or a chain of blocks where Block represents the transaction and hash of previous block.

Challenge 3

In our system, all transactions are written down and shared, but who validates the transactions?

What if John has no actual Fixed deposit and is just giving a fake document as a collateral?

Who makes sure that John really does have a fixed deposit of 20 lakh?

We solve this through a **consensus algorithm.**

A simple example could be where the majority of the anonymous people, say 51 out of the 100, must agree that the transaction is valid before it is added to the record.

The agreement is reached when more than half of the people agree that John's claim of having a 20 lakh FD is valid. This system ensures that no single individual can manipulate the transactional record. Additionally, it also demands participation and responsibility from the people.

Therefore, rather than a single person, John, claiming he has the Fixed Deposit, there is a whole network of people who will confirm it.

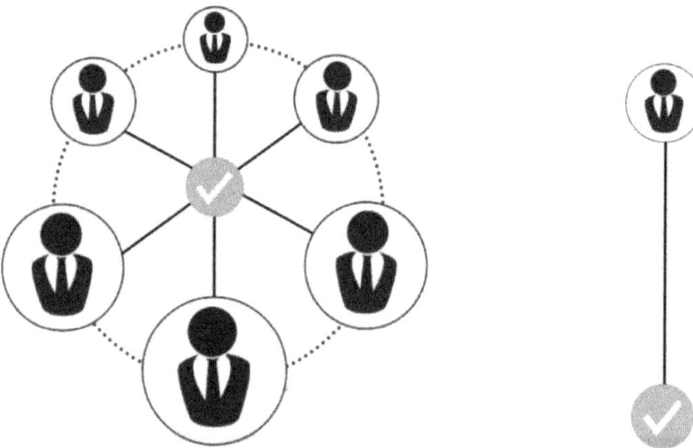

Decentralised consensus   Centralised consensus

Challenge 4

Let's look at the responsibilities of the crowd in this scenario.

1. They have to maintain a distributed ledger so they will be using their own personal storage.
2. They will spend resources to save and maintain the record such as electricity and computational power
3. They are participating in validating the transaction by participating in the consensus
4. They are the ones who help solve the conflict if it arises

Even if someone in the crowd never does any transaction in this room, they still have to do all the above steps and more.

Why would that person do it? The idea of an unbiased system is good but it is not adding any direct value to them.

Incentivization is the key here.

Every person who contributes to the network gets a reward for their participation in enabling a secured decentralized digital economy.

For a random person, they get incentives, a genuine rate of interest when needed, and a trustworthy environment.

> *"Call it what you will, incentives are what get people to work harder."*
>
> *- Nikita Khrushchev*

Challenge 5

There will be several interactions, among the borrower, the lender, and the crowd. Therefore, it becomes more important to adopt a system that ensures **complete anonymity.**

What we essentially want to achieve is that people can trust each other without revealing their identity or information.

In hindsight, that is exactly what we do with Banks. A user inputs an account number or UPI ID of the other person and send some money from their account.

In the decentralized environment, we adopt a similar model. We will assign each person a unique fixed length combination of words and numbers. This is called a cryptographic key.

Therefore, every person in the auditorium room has a cryptographic key which uniquely identifies them. Just like a roll number.

In a sense, this key is what publicly represents the person. This is also known as a public key.

Just like an account number in banks, users can have a public key on Blockchain which is the address used to send and receive money.

To access this public key records or to authenticate transactions, there is a password which is again a cryptographic key. Like any other password, this key has to be kept private and safe. This is called a private key.

Since there is a public key and a private key, an address and a password, there needs to be a vault.

A place to see and access to all the user-owned assets.

This is what we call a crypto wallet.

The key word in focus here is "See". Remember, all the assets exist on a ledger or a record which is shared with multiple people. So this wallet is just an interface that shows all the relevant records and assets a user has among the millions of records that exist on the ledger.

In summary, by incorporating public key cryptography, everyone has a pair of keys, a public key that they share with the crowd and a private key that they keep to themselves. When John wants to borrow money, he signs the transaction with his private key and shares it using his public key. Anyone can validate the transaction using John's public key, but they can't figure out John's real identity. This ensures that even though everyone knows about the transaction, the anonymity is maintained.

By overcoming these challenges, we're not just building a secure and trustworthy system, but also one that is scalable, efficient, and keeps the power with the people - a true democracy ***where Privacy and Transparency co-exist.***

Revision: The Blockchain Analogy

Imagine a blockchain as a bustling city filled with streets (peer-to-peer networks), houses (databases), and people (participants).

This city is unique because it doesn't have a single governing body like a mayor or a council; instead, the inhabitants self-govern through a shared agreement, much like distributed computing. It's also special because there's an advanced, uncrackable security system in place (cryptography), a foolproof method to keep every piece of information distinct and unchanged (hashing), and a mechanism through which every citizen agrees on shared rules and facts (consensus algorithms).

Now, let's delve into the heart of this blockchain city. The streets are the peer-to-peer networks that keep the city connected.

Every home can directly reach out to every other home, without needing to pass any central hub. This network layout removes the need for a middleman, facilitates faster communication, and reduces the possibility of a single point of failure (or is the department is on a holiday).

The city's inhabitants live in houses, which represent databases in the blockchain. Just like homes in a city store and protect personal belongings, databases in a blockchain store and secure transactional data. They also maintain an organized record of each transaction made in the blockchain city.

However, unlike the tangible brick-and-mortar houses we know, these databases are digital and exist simultaneously on every computer in the city. This distributed nature of databases forms the basis of distributed computing in blockchain, offering redundancy, and eliminating the possibility of single-point data corruption or loss.

The city's advanced security system is cryptography, the invisible shield that protects the privacy of the city's inhabitants. Like the keys to a house, every inhabitant possesses a pair of cryptographic keys: a public one, which they can share with others, akin to an address, and a private one, which they guard with their life, much like the key to their home. When one resident wants to send a message to another, they 'lock' the message with the recipient's public key just like sending a letter with their home address, and only the recipient's private key can 'unlock' and read it.

Every piece of information in this city is unique, just as every house has a distinct address. This uniqueness is ensured by hashing. Even the slightest change in any information creates a completely different hash, much like changing one digit in a house number leads you to a different house altogether.

Finally, the consensus algorithms act as the city's democratic decision-making process. Instead of a mayor making decisions, the city's inhabitants reach a consensus on the city's matters. This could be akin to agreeing on when to have a city festival, organising a kitty party, deciding society rules, and so on. Everyone's agreement ensures that the decision is fair and accepted, maintaining the order and harmony of the city.

In conclusion, just like the unique parts of a city come together to form a bustling, functioning metropolis, so do cryptography, hashing, peer-to-peer networks, consensus algorithms, distributed computing, and databases mesh together to form blockchain technology. Blockchain, much like our imaginary city, ensures a democratic, secure, and fair system where every participant has a say, and every transaction is secure and transparent.

Now imagine multiple societies in the same city, that's different Blockchain applications built on top of a Blockchain platform.

Multiple countries are multiple Blockchain platforms, connected through roads or bridges. In a similar way, there are several protocols that enable communication between different Blockchain platforms.

Chapter 3

BLOCKCHAIN ESSENTIALS

When we think about the Internet, no one talks about the underlying TCP/IP protocols but the concepts that have emerged on top of the Internet.

For instance, Emails, Social media, Online entertainment, Chats and Video calls, Websites, and even the random Google or ChatGPT search.

The world enjoys all of these activities but hardly talks about what lies underneath. The building block. The Internet.

In a similar way, Blockchain has brought many new concepts to light. These concepts have the power to transform our lives by revolutionizing the everyday processes.

Blockchain is a down-to-earth technology, it is going to be at the backend while enabling the revolution for centuries to come.

Let us go through some of the main applications or concepts that Blockchain has brought to life.

1. Smart Contracts

A smart contract is essentially a digital agreement that includes all terms and conditions agreed upon by all parties involved. It's programmed in a way that automatically executes and manages these agreed terms, eliminating the need for an intermediary.

In simpler terms, think of a smart contract like a vending machine. User inputs what they want (fulfil the conditions of the contract), and the machine automatically gives them what they requested (the contract is executed).

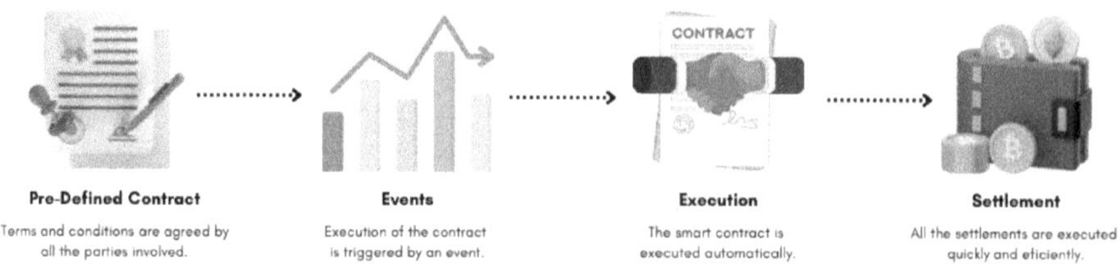

This smart contract can be implemented on a blockchain platform. Here's why it is beneficial:

- It makes the contract transparent and tamper-proof.
- Once the conditions are met, the contract executes itself.
- No one can interfere with it or stop it.

In conclusion, smart contracts are powerful tools in the digital business world, offering security, automation, and efficiency to a wide range of processes and transactions.

2. DAOs

DAO or a Decentralised Autonomous Organization is one of the oldest and proven methods of governance that has transformed with the integration of Blockchain.

Before getting into DAOs, let us go through Panchayat. Still found commonly in some parts of India, Panchayat is the perfect way to understand DAOs.

The Panchayat raj is a local government system that comes from countries like India, Pakistan, Bangladesh, Sri Lanka, and Nepal. It's one of the oldest types of local government in the area, with history going back to around 250 CE. Although the concept goes much beyond that time.

The name "Panchayat raj" is made up of two parts: "raj" means "rule," and "panchayat" means a group of five. So, it's like a rule by a group of five people.

Traditionally, Panchayats were made up of wise and respected older people chosen by the local community. They would help solve problems and disagreements between individuals and even whole villages. There were different types of these groups, but they all worked to help keep peace and order in their local areas.

After every set term, for instance one year, the villagers or the local community would vote and choose 5 people to lead the decision making and conflict resolution.

Mahatma Gandhi *wanted the panchayat raj to be the base of India's government. He wanted a* ***decentralized*** *system where each village took care of its own things. This idea was called Gram Swaraj, or "village self-governance."*

But India ended up with a more centralized government, where the main government controls most things. However, they have given some power to local village councils, called gram panchayats. This means that the local councils still have some say in what goes on in their area, which is a bit like what Gandhi had in mind.

Essentially, as global trade became more prominent and world required better governance models, Panchayats ended up being an intricate system. Establishing Panchayats specially in countries like India with densely populated demography, is challenging.

This is where Decentralized Autonomous Organizations (DAOs) come into play, and the role of blockchain technology becomes apparent.

A DAO is an organization represented by rules encoded as a computer program that is transparent, controlled by the organization members, and not influenced by a central authority. DAOs are the most effective and fair systems yet to manage collective resources.

Decentralized Autonomous Organizations (DAOs) can be seen as the new panchayats in the digital space. Just like panchayats, where local communities come together to make decisions and manage their affairs, DAOs allow people from around the world to collaborate without the need for central authorities or intermediaries. Operating on blockchain technology, DAOs create a platform where decisions are made by the members, similar to the community-driven approach of the traditional panchayats.

This democratic, transparent structure echoes the decentralized governance of panchayats, but in a global and digital context, making DAOs a modern adaptation of an age-old concept.

Understanding DAOs

Imagine a global online community that wants to support open-source software development. They decide to create a DAO that will manage funds and decide which projects to support. Everyone who wants to participate can buy a token representing a share in the DAO using cryptocurrency.

These tokens give members the right to vote on proposals about how to spend the community's funds. This is a crucial step because owning a token means that all members have some amount of money invested in the DAO. If the DAO is not working properly, their money will lose its value which enforces responsibility.

Now, let's say a developer from Canada proposes a new open-source project that needs funding. The proposal is submitted to the DAO, and all members around the world can review the details. Each member can then vote on the proposal, with their vote's weight directly tied to the number of tokens they hold.

If the proposal gains enough support, the DAO's smart contracts automatically transfer the necessary funds to the developer without needing to go through traditional banking channels or legal contracts. All actions are transparently recorded on the blockchain, ensuring accountability and trust among members.

This DAO has thus enabled a decentralized community of like-minded individuals across the globe to work together, efficiently allocate resources, and support projects they believe in, all without the need for centralized control or intermediaries. It's a powerful demonstration of the flexibility, transparency, and innovation that blockchain technology can bring to collaborative efforts.

3. Blockchain Trilemma

The Blockchain Trilemma is a concept coined within the blockchain community. According to this concept, any system or process in the world where Blockchain has to be implemented, decentralization, security, and scalability are the three major characteristics that matter.

However, with the current capabilities, it is impossible to achieve all of the three characteristics simultaneously in any one blockchain system.

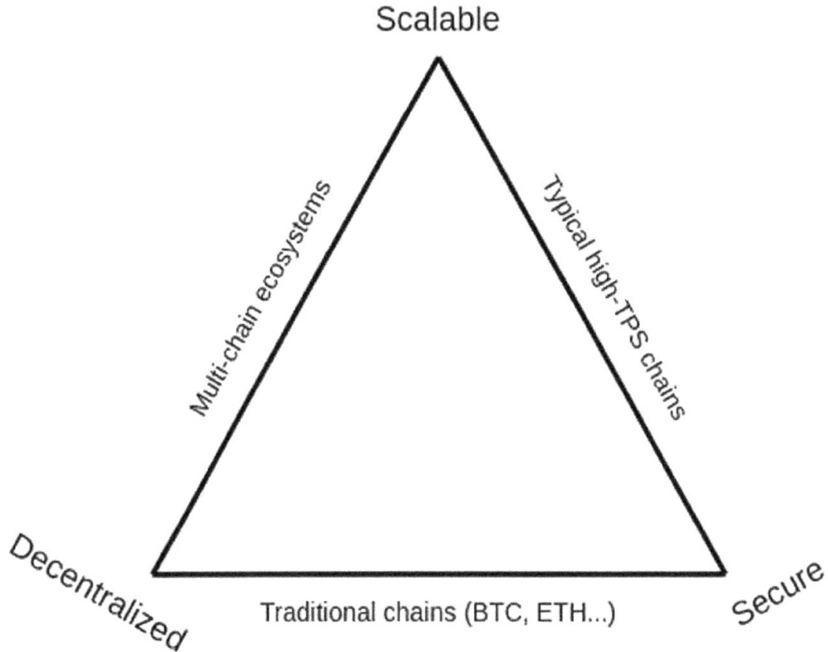

These characteristics can be laid out in the form of a triangle where each edge represents one characteristic.

In simpler terms, if a blockchain is decentralized and secure, it might struggle to handle a high number of transactions per second (TPS). This is because more cryptographic measures are used for security and more nodes will be maintaining the ledger for decentralization hence decreasing the speed, thereby falling short on scalability.

Conversely, if it's scalable and secure, it could be lesser decentralized or more centralized, leading to possible manipulation and lack of trust.

And lastly, if it's decentralized and scalable, the security aspect could be compromised, leaving the network vulnerable to attacks.

The Blockchain Trilemma thus fundamentally challenges the developers to find a delicate balance among these three vital parameters, while continuing to strive towards an innovative solution that could potentially fulfil all three at once.

Many Blockchain platforms claim to have solved the Blockchain Trilemma through various techniques.

4. Sidechains

Out of the three characteristics in the Blockchain Trilemma, Scalability in the Blockchain network has been neglected for a long time due to the priority given to decentralization and security.

However, the need for scalability has been growing exponentially in the shadows as Blockchain tries to replace the existing, highly scalable solutions.

Sidechain is one of the concepts used to achieve scalability in the Blockchain ecosystem.

What is a Side Chain?

A side chain can be thought of as a child Blockchain that is connected to the main Blockchain. In essence, a side chain is a small Blockchain that creates a separate ecosystem. The transactions or activities done inside the side chain ecosystem are pushed to the main Blockchain.

In other words, all the transactions in a side chain end up being a block in the main Blockchain. There is a two-way peg between a side chain and the main Blockchain to maintain standarization.

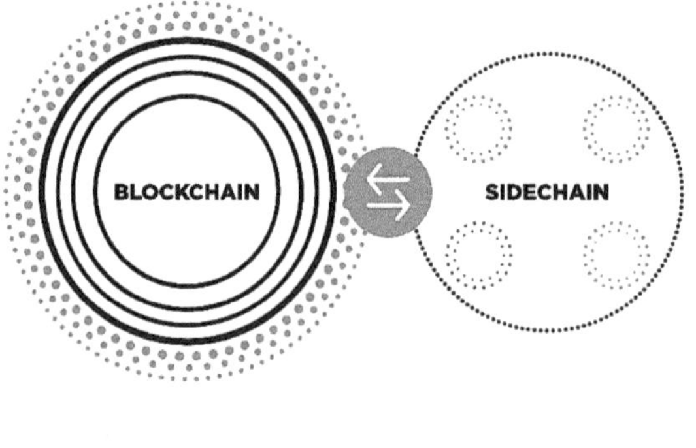

This two-way peg ensures that the side chains operate with the defined rules and regulations of the main Blockchain. With the use of side chains, traffic of the main Blockchain can be diverted, leading to lesser network congestion, more scalability, and lesser transaction fees.

5. Forks

Imagine someone on a road trip and suddenly the road splits into two. The person has to choose one way to continue their journey.

That's similar to a 'fork' in the blockchain world.

Forking in Blockchain

Orignal Blockchain

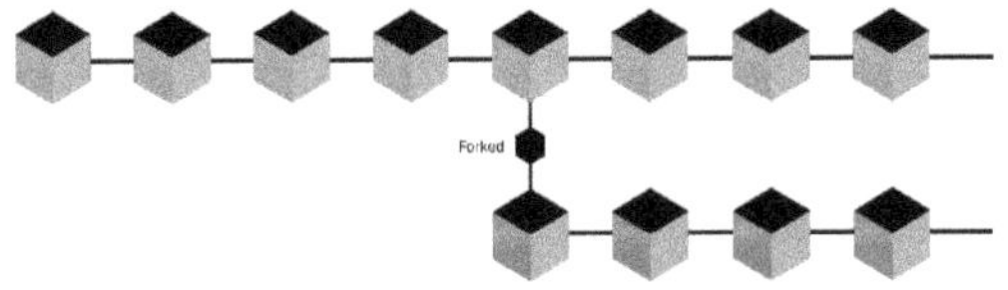

Forked Blockchain

A fork is like a divergence in the path of a blockchain. It can occur when the blockchain rules, also known as the protocol, change. When this happens, everyone in the network has to agree to these changes for them to take effect. This means that once the network agrees to certain change, the Blockchain starts operating with modifications.

For instance, the network says that we want one block to have double the size than it previously had to store more transactions in one go. Once the agreement is there, every new block in the Blockchain will have double its original size and record more transactions.

Types of Forks

There are primarily two types of forks:

Hard Fork

Hard Fork is like a drastic turn in the road which is only one way and you cannot go back if you take this road. A hard fork creates a permanent divergence from the previous version of the blockchain, and nodes running the old version will not be accepted in the new network. In hard fork, all participants must upgrade to the new version to continue participating. A hard fork can be planned (like an upgrade) or contentious (when there's disagreement within the community). An example of a hard fork is when Bitcoin Cash split from Bitcoin in 2017 due to disagreements over block size.

Another example is Ethereum and Ethereum Classic. In 2016, due to the infamous DAO hack, Ethereum underwent a hard fork to return stolen funds. However, some community members believed in the principle of immutability ("code is law") and decided not to upgrade, resulting in two separate chains - Ethereum (ETH) and Ethereum Classic (ETC).

Soft Fork

This is a gentler turn in the road and is backward compatible with the old path. This means that even if a node has not updated their blockchain software, they can still recognize and validate new blocks on the blockchain. However, to fully participate and understand the new transactions, they would need to upgrade to the new rules.

A well-known example of a soft fork in blockchain technology is the Segregated Witness (SegWit) update on the Bitcoin network to improve scalability.

In 2017, Bitcoin's developer community initiated SegWit to alleviate some of the scalability issues inherent to the original design of the Bitcoin blockchain. It accomplished this by changing how data was stored, effectively allowing more transactions to be packed into each block.

SegWit was implemented as a soft fork, meaning that nodes running the older software could still validate new transactions, ensuring backward compatibility.

This enhancement has played a significant role in helping Bitcoin scale and improving transaction efficiency on the Bitcoin network.

Remember, forks are an essential part of blockchain's ability to adapt and evolve. They're a way for communities to implement important changes and improvements to a system, or sometimes they are a result of differences in objectives or philosophies within the community.

6. Consensus Algorithms

In the world of blockchain, it is vital to keep everyone on the same page. Imagine it as a game where everyone has to agree on the rules and who scored a point. Consensus algorithm is the rulebook of the game, or in this case, the blockchain network.

The consensus protocol helps everyone in the network agree on the authenticity of the transactions. It ensures that every transaction, once confirmed, gets added to a block in the blockchain network.

The beauty of this system is that there's no boss or referee; instead, everyone gets to play a part in verifying the transactions. And because of this, it's a lot harder for any player (or user) to cheat or make false claims.

Consensus protocols are vital because they make sure that all information added to the blockchain is correct and agreed upon by everyone.

Different blockchain networks may use different consensus protocols, each with its pros and cons. Ethereum, for instance, has switched its protocol from 'Proof of Work' to 'Proof of Stake' to make transactions faster and more efficient.

In short, the consensus protocol is the ***heart of a blockchain*** *network, ensuring that all transactions are valid, agreed upon, and securely added to the blockchain. It's the unsung hero that keeps the integrity of blockchain technology intact.*

Types of Consensus Protocols

Proof of Work

The first widely known consensus protocol was Proof of Work or commonly referred to as PoW, implemented in the Bitcoin Blockchain.

The work, in Proof of Work, refers to the effort made by the computers (miners) to solve a puzzle. It's hard to find the solution to the puzzle, but once found, it's easy for everyone else on the network to verify it.

Since the mathematical puzzle is highly complex, miners need to have advanced machines to solve these puzzles. Therefore, a miner has to spend a significant amount of money in terms of resources, electricity, and time.

This tremendous effort not only validates transactions and adds them to the blockchain, but it also ensures the network's security by making it very costly in terms of time and energy to attempt fraudulent activities.

After all, if there is a fraudulent activity, it will be the miner who will incur the maximum loss.

Proof of Stake

As the name suggests, Proof of Stake or PoS consensus algorithm is based on how much stake a validator has in the network.

Most public Blockchains have their own native currencies such as ETH for Ethereum. According to Proof of Stake, a person with a significant number of the native currency on stake is allowed to validate.For instance, a person with a large number of ETH on stake, will be allowed to validate new transactions on the Ethereum network.

The reason is simple: If the validator conducts a fraudulent activity, it will lead to the crash of the network which leads to depreciating value of ETH. And since the validator has a significant amount of ETH on stake, they will be at a greater loss.

With this approach, PoS consumes significantly less computational power than PoW which is why it has become extremely popular over the last few years. Variants like pure proof of stake or delegated proof of stake have also surfaced as a better PoS structure.

Delegated Proof of Stake

In DPoS, clients can either cast a vote themselves or give this power to another client who then acts on their behalf.

Casting a vote symbolizes validating a transaction on the Blockchain network. The chosen clients are also referred to as witnesses and are responsible for making blocks by confirming the transactions.

As soon as the validators confirm and sign all the transactions in a block, they get rewards which are usually shared with their individual electors. If a validator neglects to confirm the transactions in the given time period, all the transactions are left unconfirmed and no rewards are dispersed. In such a scenario, the validator ends up losing their stake so they are obligated to confirm the transaction.

Proof of Authority

Proof of Authority (PoA) is a consensus mechanism in a blockchain network where a limited number of nodes, chosen based on their reputation and trustworthiness, are given the authority to validate transactions and add new blocks to the blockchain.

This makes the system efficient and less energy-consuming, but it also relies heavily on trust and can be more centralized than other blockchain models.

Practical Byzantine Fault Tolerance

Practical Byzantine Fault Tolerance (PBFT) is used in some blockchain networks to ensure that all nodes in the network agree on the state of the shared ledger, even if some nodes are faulty or malicious. In a PBFT system, each node in the network communicates with every other node, sharing its version of the truth.

PBFT can tolerate up to one-third of nodes being faulty or malicious without compromising the network's integrity.

The main benefit of PBFT is its ability to provide high performance and security in a network, but it requires a lot of communication between nodes, which can make it less suitable for very large networks.

Proof of Elapsed Time

PoEt works similar to the proof of work, yet burns through undeniably less power.

Proof of Elapsed Time (PoET) is a consensus algorithm that assigns block validation rights based on the concept of a fair lottery system. The main idea is that every participant in the network waits for a randomly chosen amount of time, and the one who finishes waiting first gets to validate the next block.

Rather than having members tackle a cryptographic riddle, the calculation utilizes a trusted execution environment (TEE) to guarantee blocks get delivered in an arbitrary lottery style.

Directed Acyclic Graph

Directed Acyclic Graphs (DAG) isn't a consensus algorithm itself, but a data structure that some blockchain networks use to achieve consensus in a different way than traditional blockchains.

In simple words, DAG is like a network of interconnected roads, where each point or node is a transaction. Each new transaction verifies the previous transactions, and this way, all transactions become interconnected. The 'directed' part means the roads or connections only go one way (from newer to older transactions), and 'acyclic' means you can't start at one transaction and loop back to it.

DAG does not require miners to add blocks to the chain, which saves resources and can make the network more energy-efficient. In a DAG-based system, more the transactions processed, the faster and more secure the network becomes.

Proof of Capacity

Proof of Capacity (PoC) is a consensus algorithm that allows miners to mine blocks and validate transactions based on the amount of storage space they have available on their computer. It is like a lottery where the more tickets a miner has, the higher their chances of winning. Here, each 'ticket' represents a portion of their storage space.

Therefore, with Proof of Capacity, the bigger the 'digital storage box', the better the chances of being rewarded.

Proof of History (PoH)

Proof of History (PoH) is a consensus mechanism that uses the passage of time between operations to validate transactions.

PoH maintains a sequence of cryptographic hashes - complex codes that are unique and can't be reversed. Each new event or operation gets its own unique hash, and the next one is created based on the previous hash, so there is a linked sequence that shows the exact order and timing of everything that happened.

This way, Proof of History provides a way to prove that a specific event in the network (like a transaction) occurred at a specific moment in time, without relying on other participants and without the need for extensive communication or synchronization across the network.

Ripple Protocol Consensus Algorithm

Ripple Protocol Consensus Algorithm (RPCA) is a consensus method used by Ripple's payment and exchange network. Unlike traditional consensus methods, the RPCA doesn't require all network participants to agree. Instead, it works based on trust.

In simple terms, every node (computer) on the Ripple network has a unique list of other nodes that it trusts not to defraud. This is called a Unique Node List (UNL). During each round of consensus, nodes exchange transaction data with their UNLs, and they all vote on the validity of the transactions.

If a supermajority (usually 80% or more) agree that a transaction is valid, then it becomes part of the ledger - the official record of all transactions. If they don't reach a supermajority, then the process repeats, with the nodes adjusting their votes to try to reach consensus.

The RPCA enables fast, secure transactions, with consensus reached approximately every 3-5 seconds, making it an efficient method for financial transactions.

On July 13, 2023, Ripple got a partial win against the U.S. Securities and Exchange Commission in court as a judge ruled that XRP is not a security in some cases which has accelerated its adoption among financial institutions.

7. Non-Fungible Tokens - NFTs

NFTs are assets having a unique digital presence with distinct attributes.

By using smart contracts and associating certain distinct properties, an asset can be represented on top of a Blockchain network. This asset can either be digital or physical.

Tokens on Blockchain are used to represent the ownership of the asset. Transferring these tokens represents the transfer of ownership of the asset rather than the asset itself.

These NFTs are stored on the immutable ledger of Blockchain.

Characteristics of NFTs

Indivisible

NFTs cannot be divided into smaller parts unlike fungible assets such as a 20 dollar note that can be divided into smaller units. There is a concept of partial ownership that is often confused with subdividing the NFTs but in essence, partial ownership is owning a particular share of the NFT as a whole.

Indestructible

The actual asset may be destroyed but the corresponding data of the asset that exists in Blockchain's immutable ledger is indestructible. Therefore, the asset itself stays in the Blockchain's record for as long as the Blockchain exists. A suitable example to understand this would be buying a ticket to a movie. The ticket is destroyed after the event is over but the record of who bought the ticket will always be there in the ledger.

Proof of Ownership

During the creation of an NFT, the origin of the asset gets embedded into the Blockchain ledger which provides proof of ownership. Therefore, even if a ticket is bought and sold a hundred times, the latest owner can always verify the origin of the ticket and be sure about its authenticity.

In addition to this, being Platform-specific has also emerged as a key characteristic. Since there are multiple Blockchain platforms that allow the creation of NFTs, they can be platform-specific.

Different Platforms for Creating NFTs

As mentioned in the previous paragraph, there are different Blockchain platforms that can be used to create NFTs. These NFTs are specific to the platform used and hence are non-interchangeable in most cases. This means that an NFT on Blockchain platform A cannot be transferred to Blockchain platform B.

Mentioned below are the most popular Blockchain platforms currently being used for NFT creation:

- Ethereum

- Polygon
- Avalanche
- Flow Blockchain
- WAX Blockchain
- Algorand
- Binance Smart Chain
- Polkadot
- Tezos
- Cosmos
- Near

And more.

NFTs created on the Ethereum Blockchain can belong to the smart contract standards ERC721 and ERC1155.

Recently, NFTs have been created on the Bitcoin Blockchain through an inscription process using the Ordinals protocol. Each Bitcoin NFT has a serial number, or ordinal, that is imprinted on a single satoshi (smallest unit in bitcoin currency). This unique number makes each of these digital assets rare and valuable.

8. ERC

The Ethereum Request for Comment, also abbreviated as ERC, is the overall framework approach and community building in the Ethereum environment.

Token standards such as ERC-20, ERC-721, ERC-777, to name a few, are all mentioned in the request for comment which define different standards for the token development. ERC also covers name registries, library/package formats, and several more, aside from token standards.

In short, ERC is the one that regulates the Ethereum network's entire applicability.

Some popular ERC standards are:

- **ERC-20** - A standard interface for fungible (interchangeable) tokens, like voting tokens, staking tokens or virtual currencies.

- **ERC-721** - A standard interface for non-fungible tokens, like a deed for artwork or a song.
- **ERC-777** - ERC-777 allows people to build extra functionality on top of tokens such as a mixer contract for improved transaction privacy or an emergency recover function to bail someone out if they lose their private keys.
- **ERC-1155** - ERC-1155 allows for more efficient trades and bundling of transactions – thus saving costs. This token standard allows for creating both utility tokens (such as $BNB or $BAT) and Non-Fungible Tokens like CryptoPunks.
- **ERC-4626** - A tokenized vault standard designed to optimize and unify the technical parameters of yield-bearing vaults.

Note: Scan the QR code to see all ERC token standards.

9. Stablecoins

Stablecoins are digital assets that attempt to reduce or eradicate volatility associated with cryptocurrencies by pegging to the prices of more stable assets such as fiat currencies like the US dollar or even gold. Stablecoins, despite their name, do not come without dangers for investors.

Based on the underlying assets, stable coins can be crypto-backed, Fiat-backed, commodity-backed, or algorithmic.

The most popular example of stable coins is USDT(Tether) and USDC(Circle).

10. Decentralized Finance

Decentralized Finance or DeFi is one of the crown jewels of Blockchain applications.

Decentralization (Blockchain) + Finance = DeFi

In simple words, DeFi is a concept where Blockchain is used to create a decentralized digital financial ecosystem.

In decentralized finance, financial activities are carried between individuals without the need for a third party like a bank or a financial institute.

Contrary to traditional banking system where a government issued currency is used for exchange of value, Decentralized Finance uses a digital currency to enable financial transactions.

How Does It Work?

Decentralized Financial Transaction (e.g., on the Ethereum network):

- **Initiation:** The sender decides to transfer cryptocurrency or tokens. They initiate the transaction using a crypto wallet, specifying the recipient's address (Public key), the amount, and any optional data.
- **Transaction Signing:** The sender's wallet will "sign" the transaction with their private key. This cryptographic signature proves the authenticity of the transaction.
- **Broadcast to Network:** The signed transaction is broadcasted to the cryptocurrency network and is picked up by network participants called nodes.
- **Miners/Validators Involvement:** Miners (in proof-of-work systems) or validators (in proof-of-stake systems) will pick up the transaction and include it in a block. They will validate the transaction's legitimacy, ensuring the sender has the funds and that the signature matches.
- **Consensus Algorithm:** Once the transaction is validated, it is included in a block. This block is then added to the blockchain after consensus is reached within the network.
- **Settlement:** Unlike traditional transactions, once a block is added to the blockchain (after a few confirmations to ensure security), the transaction is considered settled. The whole process can take from a few seconds to a few hours, depending on the network congestion.

- **Transaction Fees:** In decentralized systems, senders pay a fee for the network to process their transaction. This fee goes to the miners or validators. The fee can vary based on network congestion and the sender's urgency.
- **Notification:** Wallets or interfaces monitoring the blockchain can notify users when their transaction is confirmed.

Note: The currency being used in this whole system is a digital currency which is not issued by any central authority but developed through code. This currency's value is maintained by the supply and demand which again is governed by predefined code. Therefore, all network participants trust a piece of code that has been added to the Blockchain's ledger and is immutable. The code will never change unless all participants agree and therefore, all transactions will be carried out in a standard manner.

Use cases of DeFi

1. **Lending and Borrowing:** Platforms like Aave, Compound, and MakerDAO allow users to lend and borrow funds directly from others, earning interest as a lender or paying interest as a borrower.
2. **Derivatives:** Platforms such as Synthetix let users mint, trade, and bet on synthetic assets that track the value of real-world assets like stocks or commodities.
3. **Insurance:** Nexus Mutual and other platforms provide insurance services against smart contract failures or other risks.
4. **Exchanges:** Decentralized exchanges (DEXs) like Uniswap or Sushiswap allow users to trade assets peer-to-peer without trusting an intermediary.
5. **Tokenization:** Many DeFi protocols utilize tokens to represent assets or rights within the system. For instance, if you deposit Ethereum into a lending platform, you might receive a token representing your deposit and the interest you'll earn.
6. **Collateralization and Over-collateralization:** To minimize trust requirements and counteract the absence of credit scores in DeFi, many platforms require users to overcollateralize their loans. This means depositing more than what is being borrowed to ensure trust.

Chapter 4

BLOCKCHAIN AND OTHER TECHNOLOGIES

In the current world where everything is connected, the success of technology cannot be defined by its individual capabilities but by its ability to complement other technologies.

Since we established that Blockchain enables the IOS statement when it comes to data, let us see how some of the emerging technologies have an extreme dependency on data to work efficiently, making Blockchain an integral part.

Notable Intersections

- AI models learn from historical data to make predictions and decisions. The larger and more comprehensive the dataset, the better an AI model can perform. If the data is inaccurate, so is the output by the AI model.
- Quantum computers can process enormous amounts of data at once, solving complex problems faster. Their performance is directly related to the amount and quality of data they're given.
- 5G networks enable faster data transfer rates, allowing for more data-intensive applications. The network's effectiveness depends on understanding and managing data flow. The data being transferred through the 5G network needs better security.
- Autonomous vehicles use sensory data to navigate the environment safely. Their decision-making algorithms depend on constant, high-quality data input.

- Biotechnologies like genetic editing and vaccine development rely on genetic data. This data is vital to understanding and influencing biological processes and depends extensively on quality data.
- IoT devices continuously generate and process data. The functionality of these devices depends on the efficient handling of this data in terms of storage and security.

All of these statements can be labeled as a challenge in either maintaining the integrity of data, ownership of data, or security of data.

Therefore, Blockchain, with its immutable and decentralized ledger, becomes a defacto requirement or the fundamental element for the emerging digital landscape.

In the following sections, we will look into the intersection of Blockchain with three emerging technologies, AI, IOT, and Cybersecurity along with some projects that are already using this intersection.

Blockchain and AI

AI simulates human intelligence in machines, utilizing algorithms to learn from vast datasets, identify patterns, and make predictions. Its capacity for data analysis and decision-making is transformative, but the efficiency and reliability of AI models often hinge on **data quality** and **Data integrity**.

This is where blockchain comes into the picture, serving as the linchpin for highly efficient AI models.

This synergy, however, goes both ways. In many possible ways, AI can be equally important for Blockchain protocols and applications to work more efficiently. For instance, one of the key factors holding back Blockchain's ability is decision-making through consensus algorithms. This is where AI-based decision-making algorithms can help improve the speed and accuracy of a Blockchain network.

Ensuring Data Integrity

If the AI ingests incorrect or manipulated data, the model's predictions can be significantly off, leading to poor decision-making.

Blockchain's core attributes — transparency, immutability, and security — allow it to maintain the integrity of data. It provides an audit trail for each data point, ensuring that the data fed into AI models is reliable and has not been tampered with. This trustworthiness is vital in areas such as healthcare or finance, where data integrity can directly impact people's lives and well-being.

In addition to this, Blockchain's capability of maintaining privacy and transparency at the same time becomes the perfect solution for AI models.

AI models need authentic data from previous users. At the same time, the data of previous users should not be exposed to the outside world.

Therefore, AI models work on isolated data sets which are not visible to the outside world. This gives birth to several concerns such as the data sets being manipulated, the data sets being misused, or the ownership and security of these data sets.

This is often described as a "**Black Box**" problem that raises concerns over bias, fairness, and accountability and Blockchain is a natural fit for this situation.

Furthermore, recording each stage of the AI process on a blockchain can enable complete transparency of the decision-making pathway. This can enhance trust in AI systems, meet regulatory compliance needs, and facilitate the identification and rectification of AI biases or errors.

Unlocking Data Silos

AI models are data-hungry. Yet, they often face roadblocks due to data silos and privacy issues. Blockchain can dismantle these barriers and democratize data access through decentralized data marketplaces.

On a blockchain-based data marketplace, individuals can maintain control over their data while choosing to securely share or sell it. Blockchain becomes indispensable for feeding AI models with a rich, diverse data diet.

Securing AI Infrastructure

Centralized data storage within AI systems poses a significant security risk. With blockchain's decentralized and tamper-proof nature, data can be stored across multiple nodes, preventing single-point failures and protecting against data breaches.

Additionally, blockchain's encryption mechanisms can secure AI models, ensuring their integrity and preventing unauthorized access. This not only adds another layer of security but also reinforces trust in AI systems.

Blockchain in Action: AI Systems

Let us see some examples of real-life applications where Blockchain is enabling AI solutions to be more efficient.

Blackbird.AI mixes AI and blockchain to tackle the problem of fake news. Blackbird.AI uses AI to spot and categorize spam, but it's the blockchain that helps verify and build trust in the process. By using checks that are confirmed by blockchain, Blackbird.AI can figure out if a piece of news is spreading hate speech, false information, or is just a joke.

Another example of this powerful duo is Ocean Protocol that leverages the power of blockchain and artificial intelligence (AI) to democratize access to data, confronting the concerning reality of disproportionate control over data by a few powerful organizations.

In conclusion, the synergy of Blockchain and AI can create a powerful, efficient, and trustworthy environment which can transform our lives for good.

Blockchain and IOT

From healthcare to finance, agriculture to supply chain management, tolls, tickets, smart homes, and automated cars, IOT devices have made a significant impact on our lives in many ways.

Although IoT presents numerous advantages, it is not without its challenges.

The fundamental premise of the IoT is the interconnection of devices - from refrigerators, wearable health trackers to industrial sensors - all communicating and sharing information over the internet. These smart devices generate massive amounts of data, leading to the primary concern of how this data is stored, managed, and secured.

Here, blockchain comes into play.

At its core, blockchain is a distributed ledger technology (DLT) that records data across multiple devices in an immutable, transparent, and secure manner. It introduces a new method of managing and securing the vast streams of data produced by IoT devices.

Specific to the IOT devices, the main aspect of having a Blockchain integration is to replace the traditional databases and introduce a better way of storing and managing data.

Enabling IoT Reliability

In traditional, centralized IoT systems, a single point of failure can bring the whole network down, making them susceptible to outages and attacks. Blockchain's decentralized nature eliminates this risk, ensuring consistent uptime and improving the overall reliability of IoT systems.

Securing Data

Security is a paramount concern in IoT systems due to the sensitive nature of data and the proliferation of devices with various security levels. Blockchain addresses this through cryptographic algorithms that ensure data is tamper-proof once recorded. Only authorized devices with the correct cryptographic keys can access and add data to the blockchain, adding an extra layer of security that is lacking in traditional IoT systems.

Maintaining Data Integrity

The immutability of the blockchain ensures the data integrity of IoT devices. Once an entry is made on the blockchain, it is time-stamped and linked to the previous entry, making it almost impossible to alter. This prevents unauthorized modifications, ensuring the accuracy and consistency of the data.

Let us see some examples of where IOT and Blockchain are currently being used.

Blockchain in Action: IoT Systems

IBM and Maersk, a global shipping giant, teamed up to develop TradeLens, a blockchain-based solution for the global shipping industry. TradeLens leverages IoT sensors on shipping containers and blockchain to track and trace containers in real time, ensuring data integrity, reducing paperwork, and improving efficiency.

In agriculture, companies like AgriDigital use blockchain and IoT to track the farm-to-fork journey of produce. IoT devices collect data at every stage, and blockchain records it, ensuring transparency and traceability, and helping prevent food fraud.

In conclusion, the blockchain's decentralization, robust security features, and immutability make it a powerful tool to enhance IoT systems. As more IoT systems integrate with blockchain technology, we can anticipate a future where our interconnected devices are not just smarter, but also more secure and reliable.

Blockchain and Cybersecurity

Do you know -

- On October 13, 2022, 97 million people's information was stolen when Australian healthcare and insurance provider Medibank suffered a data leak.
- Prime Minister Narendra Modi's Twitter handle was "very briefly compromised" in December 2021
- Cybersecurity Ventures predicts cybercrime will cost $10.5 trillion annually by 2025.
- 94% of organizations experienced a cyberattack of some form in the year 2022
- What these data points show is the increasing demand for a better system that is resilient to cybercrime.

Cybercrime is like a disease and whenever we talk about a disease, prevention is better than cure.

Cybersecurity presents several challenges, including securing data, protecting system integrity, preventing unauthorized access, and maintaining user privacy. Blockchain can play a significant role in addressing these issues.

Let us go through the top 3 ways in which Blockchain can strengthen cybersecurity practices.

1. Enhanced Data Security and Integrity

Blockchain's inherent cryptographic algorithms ensure that data is stored in a tamper-resistant and encrypted format. This robust security measure drastically reduces the risk of data breaches, as all data modifications require the consensus of all network participants. As such, unauthorized alterations or fraudulent activities become computationally intensive, if not practically impossible.

Moreover, once a transaction has been recorded on the blockchain, it becomes permanent. The immutability of the blockchain ensures the integrity of the data, making it an excellent tool for maintaining secure logs and evidence for digital events. This tamper-proof nature provides a level of data security and assurance that traditional systems struggle to match.

2. Eliminating Single Point of Failure

Conventional cybersecurity infrastructures often rely on centralized models, where a single authority controls and manages data. These systems are vulnerable as they offer a single point of failure; if the central authority is compromised, the entire system is at risk. The Twitter hack of 2021 is the perfect example of this statement.

Blockchain's decentralized architecture distributes data across numerous nodes, eliminating this single point of failure. Since the blockchain is not controlled by a central authority, an attack would need to compromise more than half of the blockchain's nodes simultaneously to manipulate the system, an incredibly unlikely scenario due to the computational power required. This makes the blockchain infrastructure incredibly resilient to cyber threats.

3. Improved Identity Management and Authentication

Traditional methods of identity management and authentication, such as username-password combinations, are often subject to breaches, phishing, and identity theft. Blockchain can enhance identity management by providing a decentralized, universal, and tamper-proof system of record for digital identities.

With blockchain, users can have digital identities linked to their biometrics or other secure information. Access to this identity can be controlled by a private key known only to the user, significantly reducing the risk of identity theft. In addition, this identity can be used across various platforms, reducing the need for maintaining multiple usernames and passwords, a common source of security vulnerabilities.

The traditional challenges of phishing and fraud are still possible as they are associated with individual decisions and manipulation. However, Blockchain eliminates the possibility of the whole network suffering due to the mistake of one.

With more advanced Blockchain solutions like Zero-Knowledge Proof (explained in Chapter 6), the digital system becomes much more efficient. With such technology integrations, users can prove their identity without revealing any details, without even telling their names.

Therefore, Blockchain integration allows ***privacy and transparency to co-exist.***

Blockchain in Action: Cybersecurity Solutions

Blockchain has already started making a substantial impact on cybersecurity.

REMME is a blockchain-based solution that replaces traditional logins with SSL certificates stored on a blockchain, eliminating the need for password authentication, a common target for cyber attacks.

Another noteworthy example is Guardtime, which uses a blockchain system called Keyless Signature Infrastructure (KSI) to verify the integrity of data in real-time, enabling faster detection of malware and other cyber threats.

In conclusion, the incorporation of blockchain technology in cybersecurity strategies is poised to revolutionize the way we protect our digital infrastructures. With its decentralized structure, immutability, and advanced cryptographic techniques, blockchain offers a robust and resilient solution to numerous cybersecurity challenges. As we continue to explore and develop this technology further, we can look forward to a future of enhanced digital security and privacy.

Chapter 5

THE SUPPLY CHAIN CASE STUDY

Supply chain is the most overly used case studies but there is no sector more appropriate to understand the all aspects of Blockchain and the change it can bring.

Supply chain is one of the oldest systems known to mankind. From simple trade routes for exchanging goods like spices, silk, and precious metal, to the modern day complex network, Supply chain is the bedrock of global economy.

The morning coffee, the mobile phones, air conditions, even the smallest kitchen utensil is available because of the supply chain network.

However, as societies grew and technologies advanced, the supply chain became more complex. Orchestrating the flow of goods, these chains involve multiple entities such as producers, suppliers, transporters, sellers, and warehouses. Each product ushers in its own set of interactions that must adhere to standardized protocols. The vastness of these networks often means crossing international borders, which introduces various compliance and legal hurdles.

Consequently, there has been a pressing need to revolutionize the supply chain, aiming for enhanced optimization and standardization. Despite the advent of the Internet and digital advancements, the supply chain domain has, until recently, remained relatively untouched by the full spectrum of modern technological benefits.

This is where Blockchain comes in.

As discussed repeatedly in this book, there are several characteristics that Blockchain can introduce.

A supply chain is one of a few examples where all of the Blockchain's benefits can be discovered. Therefore, supply chain also becomes the perfect case study to understand the magnitude of Blockchain implementation as well as its benefits.

In the following sections, we will be taking the example of an agriculture supply chain to understand the argument further.

Agricultural Supply Chain and Blockchain

Let us assume an agriculture supply chain where a farmer in India is growing potatoes which will be exported to the United States of America.

Please remember that the use of Blockchain in a supply chain network depends on the requirement, business aspect, and the need defined by the client or the system. In this case study, we will explore all possibilities of how Blockchain can be used at various stages of a supply chain network.

Preface

A company in the US reaches out to a farmer in Punjab named Tejpal. The company proposes that if Tejpal can grow 100 KGs of X quality of potatoes, the company will buy it from him at a rate of 12 Rs. per KG whereas if Tejpal goes to the market and sells his produce, he gets 8 Rs. per KG. Therefore, Tejpal agrees to the terms and conditions of the company.

Both the farmer and the company have a public key on Blockchain through which they interact.

The company sends an agreement to Tejpal outlining the terms and conditions.

In traditional ways, this agreement takes a long time and a lot of paper work along with manual intervention.

On Blockchain, the farmer views the agreement on a digital platform and signs with his private key. This agreement is in the form of a smart contract. Therefore, on each condition, either completed or uncompleted, a certain action is executed automatically.

We will come back to this agreement multiple times in our example.

Step 1

Tejpal signs the agreements that sits on a Blockchain ledger. This agreement cannot be changed by either party and entitles Tejpal to 12 Rs. per KG if he produces the right quality of potatoes as asked by the company.

Step 2

A scientific researcher evaluates the soil quality, seed quality, water, and other factors before Tejpal starts growing the potatoes. This evaluation is recorded on Blockchain for the purpose of transparency.

Step 3

Tejpal needs a loan from the bank to invest in his produce so he can grow a quality crop. The bank verifies the agreement on the Blockchain and directly disburses the loan amount to Tejpal. In a traditional scenario, the banks have to verify the farmer, the company, and the agreement which takes a long time.

Step 4

After receiving the funds, Tejpal starts growing the crops. There is a possibility of a natural disaster like floods, hurricane, or even heavy rainfall that can destroy the crops.

In this step, the insurance provider does not just take a small premium but a fixed percentage from the farmer on successful produce. In case of any natural calamity, the smart contract on the Blockchain automatically deducts appropriate amount from the insurance provider's account and gives it to the bank to repay the loan that Tejpal took.

The purpose of making this process automatic is to enforce responsibility and promptness. In case of successful sale, the insurance company receives the promised share through smart contracts, directly in their account.

Step 5

After the potatoes are grown and harvested, the scientific researcher again evaluates the produce and adds his findings on the Blockchain ledger. This ensures that at each step, the quality of the produce is recorded on the immutable ledger of the Blockchain.

There are three reasons for recording this quality at every step:

- Enforce responsibility
- Enforce ownership
- Enforce transparency

Step 6

After the produce is harvested and evaluated, it is loaded in trucks. This is where transport company is involved. The transport company is employed by the US company to take the produce to the warehouse before exporting it.

Here, the US company will do a digital contract with the transport company through smart contracts, making the process smooth and easy.

In the agreement, the US company takes responsibility for any naturally calamity that affects the produce' quality such as accident, storm, and others.

On the other hand, any negligence by the transport company such as fault in engine or inefficient machines to store the potatoes, or any possible scenario, the transport company will be held liable to pay back to the US company.

Both the parties in this case can get insurance but it is their choice. In any case, both of them are enforced to be more responsible. Since smart contracts are involved, the debit and credit of money happens automatically based on the conditions defined.

Traditionally, the farmer suffers in such scenarios as both parties deny to pay for the damages and farmer does not get paid because no one is able to establish what went wrong and whose fault it was.

However, in this case, with Blockchain enabling transparency, immutability, and smart contract-based execution, the farmer will be paid as soon as the produce leaves the farm.

Generally, in more than 90% of the cases today whether private or government-backed systems, farmers get paid weeks or months after the produce leaves their farm. No one questions this old unfair system. In many cases, farmer is paid only after the produce is sold. If the produce gets sold for a great profit, farmer gets the same promised amount. But if the produce is sold at a loss, farmer shares the losses.

In a Blockchain based scenario, farmer will get the money in his account the same day when the produce leaves his farm after evaluation.

Step 7

Removing manipulation and bribery becomes easier with Blockchain. Since it enforces ownership, no one can even think of manipulating the system.

For instance, if the farmer wants to bribe the scientific evaluator to sell his produce, the truck from the transport company has its own evaluator who verifies the quality of the produce before loading it on the truck.

Moreover, since Blockchain is used where the identity of the involved personnel is not known, it is impossible to coordinate and manipulate the system. On the other hand, even the US company that has employed all the actors is unable to manipulate the system.

Step 8

The truck has IOT devices installed. These IOT devices will be transmitting real time data of the condition of the potatoes. The data, being stored on Blockchain, becomes the most reliable source of information to keep transparency in the network.

The transport company therefore needs to be more vigilant on maintaining the IOT devices.

Step 9

The truck reaches the warehouse. The warehouse, again, asks for an evaluation of the produce before storing it.

Generally, this is where most manipulations happen through the possible scenarios:

- The transport company delays the produce delivery and the cost of the produce can vary drastically.
- The warehouse and transport company do not notify the delivery.
- The warehouse company performs hoarding, keeping produce in store to manipulate supply and demand in the market.

- The warehouse company has not maintained its store so the produce gets affected and the farmer pays.

And more such scenarios.

However, in our case, the warehouse company has to check and update the quality of produce it receives. It knows that a similar check will be made by the next party so the company has to maintain utmost levels of quality to ensure that it does not get penalised.

Furthermore, since the transport company had to notify that it received the produce from the farmer, they will not be able to delay delivery and hence the warehouse company notifies as well.

Step 10

On the Blockchain network, it is now established that the warehouse received 100 KGs of Potatoes on a particular date and time, eliminating the possibility of manipulating supply and demand.

Since everything is transparent, price surge and hoarding are impossible to do without repercussions. Even if the proper law is not enforced, the end consumer, the farmer, and the company in US will be aware of the situation and hence choose not to work with warehouse in the future.

Step 11

The warehouse supplies the produce to the exporter who again evaluates the produce before receiving.

The exporter generally suffers from a lethargic process of custom clearing which gets simplified through Blockchain.

The importer in the US, the shipping company, the banks issuing the credit line, the agreement between the US company and the farmer, everything resides on Blockchain which can be easily evaluated by the customs team to issue permissions. The process that takes days and weeks can now be done in minutes with complete trust and robustness.

Step 12

Handling the trade finance

What is Trade Finance?

Trade finance refers to the financial instruments and products used to facilitate international trade and commerce. It bridges the gap between importers and exporters by providing various short-term credit solutions that assist in the transaction process. Trade finance aims to mitigate the risks associated with global trade, such as currency fluctuations, political instability, and the non-fulfillment of contractual obligations.

If we observe the current Trade Finance structure and analyse the foundational features of Blockchain, there can't be a better match and the ongoing initiatives in this space are the proof. Adding trust and regulation to the network, Blockchain is the catalyst for the step towards a completely digital economy.

The Basic Scenario

Since our produce is going from India to the United States, there needs to be an importer and an exporter. Someone in the US will receive the goods and then deliver to the US company. Other party will be in India who will receive the produce and transport it across borders.

The importer and exporter agree on the required terms and conditions in the form of a digital agreement, signed through their private keys on the Blockchain.

As a part of this agreement, the importer needs to ensure the exporter that the payment will be completed in full after the goods are received and exporter needs to ensure that the goods will be exported in the perfect condition.

All of this is included in the smart contract and is enforceable. After the agreement is completed, exporter sends out the goods maybe through a shipment.

Here comes bill of lading which is uploaded as a legal verified document. This document is shared between all the parties involved in the trade. It bears witness to the fact that a certain step has been accomplished and there is full transparency between the parties.

As a result, the importer is constantly informed about the status of the goods with absolute certainty. As for the payment process, importer's bank issues a letter of credit to exporter's bank ensuring the payment will be completed if the set terms are met.

These banks will also be a part of the Blockchain network.

Therefore, even the history of the importer and exporter depicting their efficiency and authenticity will be available to achieve utmost trust. Moreover, during the issuance of letter of credit (LoC), the banks will have a digital medium to securely share the document along with the most critical facility of achieving regulation and compliance through this digital medium only.

In this case, the banks are international and are connecting across border. Generally, such interactions take days if not weeks to establish authenticity and verify the details. On Blockchain, since everything is recorded in an immutable ledger after verification, the process becomes highly optimized.

From verification, validation to the issuance of the LoC, the whole process is completed through the consensus mechanism of the Blockchain in just a few hours.

Further, the network also includes a digital notary. It is responsible for various tasks such as verifying the digital signature of the participants which means that without revealing their true identity and without sacrificing trust, a trade can be completed.

Finally, the cross-border payment between the banks will be carried out more efficiently and swiftly without the need for international regulations which usually delay the existing tedious process even further.

Major Technical Perspectives

Apart from the basic use case, let's look at the most prominent aspects of a typical Trade Finance process undergoing major intensification with the advent of Blockchain, and get a technical overview of how it is actually happening.

Letter of Credit

At its core, letter of credit is a piece of paper which provides a guarantee that a third party will process the payment to the trader on behalf of the buyer provided that the trade meets some predefined conditions.

In a traditional Trade Finance process, issuing a letter of credit is a hefty task. It takes days to complete one letter of credit and considering that the whole trade depends on an authenticated and assured payment, it delays the process.

By bringing all the parties on a digital platform, the whole process of issuing LoC can be completed in just a few hours as compared to days.

For the regulations, the digital notary works as the traditional notary in providing validation to the documents and maintains a record for complete auditability.

Furthermore, the transactions carried out on the blockchain platform are direct which means there is no involvement of a third party and hence there is a considerable reduction in the transaction cost.

In April 2023, Citi India, one of the top banks in the country, successfully completed a Blockchain enabled Letter of Credit transaction on Contour, a decentralized platform.

IoT and Blockchain

The integration of IoT has also been a key consideration in the modernisation of Trade Finance. IoT devices can be used to deliver real-time information of the goods such as location and movement or in simple terms, to monitor the goods.

But the data provided by IoT needs to be monitored too and it has to be ensured that the data is not tampered with. This leads to the involvement of Blockchain.

By creating an immutable ledger where all the data is saved in the form of a record and shared with every participant, Blockchain makes sure that no one can modify the data. If we consider a scenario where 5 tons of goods has been sent by the trader and only 4 tons are received by the buyer, the IoT data on Blockchain can indicate - what went wrong, where it went wrong, and by whom.

Step 13

Finally, after the transport and warehouse process is executed in a similar way at the end of the US company, the goods reach their destination.

However, in the whole case study, there has been a constant need to authenticate the identity of a person.

The identity verification or the KYC process is omnipresent, not just in supply chain but everywhere in the world. Therefore, in the next chapter, will be looking at one of the most exciting concepts - the Zero Knowledge proof and how it enables smooth and secure identity verification globally.

Chapter 6

ZERO KNOWLEDGE PROOF

What is ZKP

In 1985, three researchers - Silvio Micali, Shafi Goldwasser, and Charles Rackoff - introduced a new idea called "knowledge complexity". This became the foundation for Zero Knowledge Proof or ZKP.

Think about ZKP like a magic trick. Suppose you're a magician (the "prover") and you have a secret trick you want to show off to your friend (the "verifier"). You want your friend to believe you've done the magic trick, but you don't want to reveal how you did it. That's the essence of ZKP.

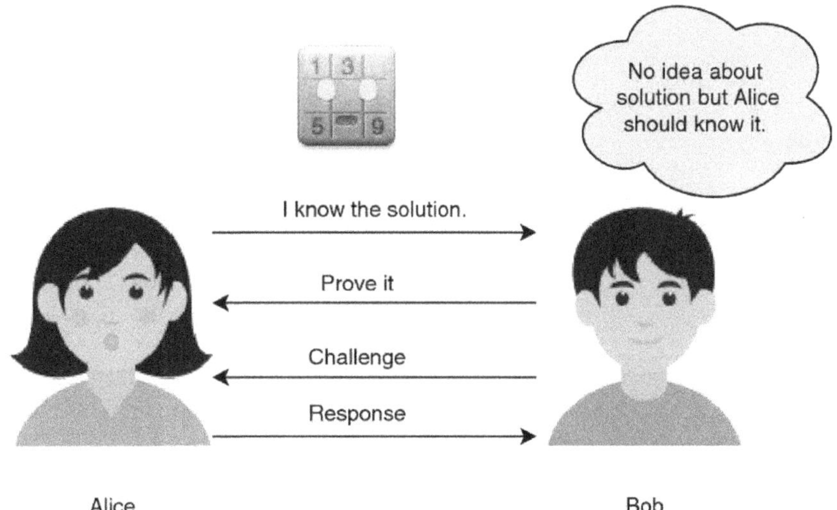

In a more technical context, ZKP is a way for one party to prove to another that they know a value (like a secret), without conveying any information apart from the fact that they know the secret.

This means a person can prove they know something or have done something without giving away any details or secrets. They don't need passwords or sensitive information. There is no risk of information getting tampered with or misused.

For example, ZKP can be used in a situation where a person wants to prove to a website that they know their password, without actually sending their password over the Internet.

ZKP is like a trustless trust - it allows two parties to trust each other without revealing their secrets. This offers a whole new level of security and privacy, making it a powerful tool in fields like cryptography and blockchain technology.

In essence, the beauty of ZKP lies in its simplicity: proving knowledge without revealing the knowledge itself.

Continuing the example in the last chapter, we will discuss how ZKP can be used to implement the Letter of Credit involving a bank in the US, a bank in India, an importer, an exporter, customs of both countries, insurance provider, and transporter.

Specifically, we will see how SNARGs, a not so common type of ZKP will be suitable for such a use case.

We will discuss how, without revealing their true identity, all the parties can establish unparalleled trust and execute a global trade.

LoC with SNARGs

Leveraging the privacy-preserving capabilities of SNARGs, we propose a model that facilitates secure, private, and transparent transactions, particularly between US and Indian trades.

SNARGs Overview: Briefly, SNARGs allow for compact, non-interactive proofs of computational integrity. They can efficiently demonstrate knowledge of a solution to a problem without revealing the solution itself.

Outcomes

1. **Enhanced Trust:** All parties can be assured of the authenticity of the trade without having the nitty-gritty of each transaction.
2. **Reduced Frauds:** Tamper-proof records, coupled with SNARG verification, reduce the possibility of fraudulent activities.
3. **Efficiency:** The need for constant verification and data exchanges between parties reduces, thanks to the non-interactive nature of SNARGs.
4. **Privacy Protection:** Crucial information remains confidential, addressing concerns of data theft or misuse.

Challenges: Implementing a new system across countries requires standardization, training, and a shift from traditional methods. Further, computational overhead, though minimized, still exists.

Let's see step by step how SNARGs will be implemented here:

The Process

Generation of Proof

Whenever an action is taken by any party, for instance, the exporter shipping a consignment, they will produce a proof using their cryptographic identity and the details of the action.

This proof asserts something like: "I am the exporter, and I have shipped the consignment." However, the proof does not reveal the identity of the exporter or the consignment details directly.

Verification of Proof

The receiving party (e.g., the importer's bank) receives the SNARG proof related to the action.

The bank then verifies the proof using the previously established public parameters. This process will confirm the authenticity of the action without revealing the specifics of the involved party or the action details.

Feedback to Stakeholders

Once verified, the bank updates the LC's status and provides feedback to the involved parties about the status of the transaction.

If the proof is invalid or there are inconsistencies, the bank can raise an alert or ask for further clarifications.

Chain of Trust

As subsequent actions are taken (e.g., customs clearance, insurance claim), new proofs are generated and verified.

This creates a chain of trust where each link is a SNARG-verified action, ensuring that the entire process remains transparent and trustworthy, ***where privacy and transparency co-exist.***

Secure Archiving

All proofs and their verifications can be securely archived, potentially on a blockchain or another immutable ledger.

This ensures that there's an indisputable record of all actions, adding another layer of trust to the system.

Conclusion of Transaction

Once all conditions of the LC are met, the bank processes the payment. Since each step was verified using SNARGs, the bank can be confident in the authenticity of the transaction and the involved parties.

Review and Audit

For any future disputes or reviews, the bank can revisit the archived proofs and verifications. This ensures that even in hindsight, the process remains transparent and verifiable without compromising on data privacy.

Types of ZKP

Zero-Knowledge Proofs (ZKPs) can be classified into several types based on their properties and use cases. Here are some of the most prominent types:

Interactive Zero-Knowledge Proofs

Interactive ZKPs require interaction between the prover and the verifier. The prover sends the proof, the verifier sends a challenge, and the prover sends a response. This back-and-forth continues until the verifier is convinced.

An example is the classic protocol between Peggy (the Prover) and Victor (the Verifier) in the cave scenario, also known as the Ali Baba cave.

Note: Scan this QR code to know more about the Ali Baba cave example that explains Interactive ZKP.

NIZKP

Non-Interactive Zero-Knowledge Proofs require only a single round of communication. The prover generates a proof by themselves and sends it to the verifier.

The verifier can check the proof without any further interaction with the prover. This property makes NIZKPs very useful in digital signatures, e-cash, and other similar applications.

zk-SNARKs

Zero-Knowledge Succinct Non-Interactive Argument of Knowledge are a form of NIZKPs that are succinct (short and easy to verify) and argument of knowledge (proofs that work computationally). zk-SNARKs are extensively used in Zcash, a privacy-focused cryptocurrency.

zk-STARKs

Zero-Knowledge Succinct Transparent Argument of Knowledge or zk-STARKs are similar to zk-SNARKs but don't require a trusted setup. They provide a higher degree of quantum-resistance and are transparent, meaning there's no hidden information. However, zkSTARKS are larger in size and more computationally intensive to produce.

Bulletproofs

Bulletproofs are a non-interactive zero-knowledge proof protocol with very short proofs and without a trusted setup. Bulletproofs are used for confidential transactions (hiding transaction amounts) in cryptocurrencies like Monero.

Sigma Protocols

Sigma is a type of interactive zero-knowledge proof where there are exactly three rounds of communication - a commitment, a challenge, and a response.

VPD

Verifiable Polynomial Delegation or VPD is a method that allows someone to prove they've done a specific mathematical task correctly without revealing all the details about how they did it. It's about having a way to quickly verify that a particular function's outcome is right, without re-doing the whole calculation.

SNARG

Succinct Non-interactive ARGuments or SNARG is a technique that gives a short and straightforward proof for a statement's truth. Instead of showing all the steps in their work, someone can provide a concise confirmation that their result is correct, and others can trust and verify this proof easily.

ZK Rollups

ZK Rollups are a scaling solution for blockchains. They bundle or "roll up" multiple transactions into a single transaction.

The technique of zk Rollups is used to validate transactions off-chain and then submit a proof to the main chain, ensuring security while boosting transaction throughput.

Optimistic Rollups

Optimistic Rollups are another scaling solution. Instead of using zero-knowledge proofs like ZK Rollups, they take an "optimistic" approach. When transactions are rolled up and submitted to the main chain, they are assumed to be valid unless challenged. If someone believes a transaction is false, they can flag it. If the challenge is valid, the incorrect transaction is removed and penalties are applied.

This approach allows for faster and more scalable processing, with the trade-off being a delay in finality until the challenge period passes.

Each type of ZKP has its pros and cons and is useful for different kinds of applications depending upon the specific requirements of the system where they're being used.

Chapter 7

ASSET TOKENIZATION

Asset tokenization is the process of converting the rights to a tangible or intangible asset into a digital token on a blockchain. This digital representation carries the value of the underlying asset and can be bought, sold, or traded on various digital platforms. By transforming physical assets into digital tokens, the ownership, purchase, and trading of these assets become more transparent, efficient, and accessible.

In the context of blockchain technology, the tokenized asset's ownership information, as well as any transactions related to it, are recorded on a secure, immutable ledger. This ensures that all parties involved have an accurate and consistent view of the ownership status and history of the asset.

What is a Token

Tokens represent a unit of value issued on a blockchain. They can symbolize various assets or rights, managed through the blockchain's decentralized ledger system.

Tokens on a blockchain are secured by the underlying network's cryptography, and ownership is determined by possession of the corresponding private key.

This facilitates peer-to-peer transactions without the need for intermediaries and provides a transparent and immutable record of ownership and transactions.

Tokens can be created through smart contracts. These smart contracts define the rules and functionality of the tokens, including how they are transferred, how transactions are approved, how users can access their balance, and how new tokens are created or minted.

The token management and access is usually done through a wallet that holds the public and private keys of the owner. The public key in the wallet is linked to the token on the Blockchain while the private key is used to authenticate any activity to be done on the token.

Types of Tokens

Tokens can be classified into two categories - utility tokens and security tokens.

Utility Tokens

Utility tokens are used to facilitate financial activities in a particular ecosystem. They serve a defined utility. For instance, we go to a theme park and buy tickets to enjoy various rides inside that theme park. In a similar sense, a utility token is used inside a digital ecosystem for various activities.

Security Tokens

Security tokens are the digital representation of a security. Security tokens come in different flavors as they can represent different securities.

The most prominent types of security tokens are:

- **Equity tokens** - Equity tokens are stocks on Blockchain. Just as traditional stocks represent the equity in a company, equity tokens are used to implement the same concept with the only difference being that these tokens are stored, issued, and managed on the Blockchain network, supercharged with trust and transparency along with a lower processing fee.

- **Debt tokens** - Tokens used to represent debt instruments such as real estate mortgages and corporate bonds on a Blockchain network are called debt tokens. To eradicate the risks such as debt default or dramatic changes in the valuation, smart contracts used to issue these debt tokens can be programmed to include certain rules such as repayment terms.
- **Derivate tokens** - These tokens derive their value from another token or an underlying asset. The underlying asset goes through a verification process to establish the ownership and then the user receives tokens having equal value as the asset. These tokens can be used for various purposes such as for getting a loan or trading.
- **Hybrid convertible tokens** - Hybrid tokens, as one might presume, cannot be made by mixing any two token types. These tokens are generally a mix of debt and equity tokens, convertible in either of them.
- **Real asset tokens** - These are used to represent the ownership of real-life assets on a Blockchain platform. Real asset tokens are the most significant types of tokens in the current digital landscape and are believed to bring significant transformation. They are used to represent assets such as commodities, real estate, and art.

Asset-backed Tokens

Tokenization of assets is bringing true digitalization. Through this digitalization, real-life assets have been exposed to a plethora of benefits including more liquidity, better visibility, traceability, lower processing fee, easy ownership transfers, and exposure to a global market.

Let us take three prominent assets and understand how tokenizing these assets is the future of our world economy:

1. **Real estate tokens:** Real estate, the largest asset class in the world, is also one of the most coarse segments. Tokenization of real estate comes as a natural solution to provide functionalities such as fractional ownership and increased market participation. Further, this also provides more liquidity which allows the sector to grow at an unprecedented rate.

2. **Gold-backed tokens:** What if the gold in our houses or in our lockers was not just sitting there but giving us instant returns? A commodity like gold can be tokenized on the Blockchain and those tokens can then be used to either lend money to other people or get loans or for numerous other reasons. It introduces new marketing opportunities and improves the trading lifecycle. It further removes the influence of institutional investors or other central authorities.
3. **Carbon credits as tokens:** Tokenization is often thought of as a way to provide more liquidity but the tokenization of carbon credits is the perfect example of how much more it can do. Using tokens to represent carbon credits allows more security and trackability. Compared to the traditional scenario where user can only access their carbon credits, tokenization allows a user to even hold or trade these credits.

The Tokenization Procedure

Mentioned below are the steps that a person, Mary, might take when trying to create tokens for an asset

Step 1: Asset Identification & Appraisal

- First, Mary selects the asset to tokenize, which could be anything from real estate, art, company equity, to any tangible or intangible value.
- Mary then arranges for a professional valuation to determine its market value, which helps in deciding the number and value of each token.

Step 2: Legal Framework & Due Diligence

- Mary must define the ownership rights associated with the token concerning the physical asset.
- It's crucial for her to ensure that the tokenization process and the subsequent sale or transfer of tokens comply with the relevant local and international regulations.

Step 3: Choosing the Token Standard on Ethereum

- Mary selects the appropriate standard on Ethereum. ERC-20 caters to fungible assets (like stocks), whereas ERC-721 is for non-fungible or unique assets (like a specific artwork).

Step 4: Smart Contract Development

- Using Ethereum's programming language, Solidity, Mary develops a smart contract that will dictate the token's behavior.
- She must incorporate features such as total supply and rules for transferring ownership, among others. Before final deployment, she tests this contract in Ethereum's test environments like Rinkeby or Ropsten to ascertain its functionality and security.

Step 5: Token Minting

- Mary deploys the contract to the Ethereum mainnet, incurring a gas fee in the process. Once active, the contract then 'mints' or creates the tokens based on the determined value.
- *Gas fee on Ethereum refers to the amount a user pays to execute a transaction or run a smart contract on the network. The term "gas" is used metaphorically using the function of energy in powering operations in the physical world to explain the function of gas in powering computations and transactions on the blockchain.*

Step 6: Token Sale/Distribution

- Mary might launch an initial offering for investors to buy these tokens. For regulatory adherence, she might also implement KYC/AML checks to verify the identity of potential buyers.

Step 7: Secondary Market & Liquidity

- For liquidity, she can opt to list the tokens on cryptocurrency exchanges or decentralized trading platforms, allowing users to buy or sell the tokens.

Step 8: Management & Reporting

- If the tokenized asset requires ongoing management, like real estate, a designated entity is chosen to manage it. Token holders may then receive regular reports or dividends based on income distributions from the asset.

Step 9: Redemption Process

- Mary might have a procedure in place where token holders can opt to convert their tokens back to the underlying asset or a proportionate share of its monetary value.

Step 10: Continuous Monitoring

- It becomes essential to monitor and update the smart contract periodically to counteract any vulnerabilities or to introduce new features or adhere to changing regulatory requirements.

Key Takeaways

- The process of tokenization democratizes asset ownership, allowing for smaller, divisible shares of an asset to be owned and traded by individuals globally.
- Marrying traditional asset management with blockchain technology requires expertise in both fields.
- As with any investment, risks are involved, and potential investors should be well-informed before purchasing tokenized assets.

Benefits of Tokenization

1. **Enhanced Liquidity:** Makes illiquid assets more accessible and tradeable through fractional ownership.
2. **Security & Transparency:** Offers an immutable, transparent record of ownership on the blockchain.
3. **Cost Efficiency & Speed:** Reduces intermediaries and facilitates faster, cross-border transactions.
4. **Democratization of Investment:** Lowers investment barriers, enabling broader participation and diversification.

5. **Programmability & Automation:** Utilizes smart contracts for automated processes and customizable token features.

Bonus sections: Tokenomics

Tokenomics, or token economics, refers to the structure and policies governing the distribution, ownership, and value of digital tokens within a blockchain ecosystem.

It's a critical aspect of cryptocurrency projects, laying out the rules for how tokens are created, distributed, and utilized. Tokenomics helps in defining the total supply of tokens, the method of distribution (such as through Initial Coin Offerings or Initial Dex Offering), and the incentives for network participation.

It may also include strategies for maintaining token supply and demand to drive value, governance rights accorded to token holders, and rules for token burning or staking.

Understanding tokenomics is essential for investors, developers, and users, as it affects the token's utility, demand, supply, and consequently, its value within the marketplace. Overall, tokenomics serves as the economic framework that guides the functioning, growth, and sustainability of a decentralized network or application.

Chapter 8

CHOOSING THE RIGHT BLOCKCHAIN PLATFORM

In the previous chapters, we discussed the gravity of the IOS statement: establishing Integrity, Ownership, and Security in data-driven ecosystem. Various case studies and real-life examples defined the profound significance of Blockchain in bringing this triad to life in the most efficient manner.

With data being considered as the new oil, the necessity of integrating Blockchain is certain.

However, selecting the right Blockchain platform is a critical decision for any individual or organization. The right choice enables the seamless integration, scalability, and functionality required to meet the business's unique demands.

There are a lot of Blockchain platforms available in the market. Each with its distinct features. Therefore, it is not a choice to be made lightly but a strategic decision which takes several parameters in consideration.

How to Choose a Blockchain

Types of Blockchain

X

Layers of Blockchain

X

Different characteristics

Combined together, these factors make it extremely difficult for any decision maker to choose the right Blockchain platform for their use case.

In an unconventional sense, choosing the right Blockchain platform is similar to finalizing which car.

In the following section, we will compare the decision of buying a car with the decision of selecting the right Blockchain platform.

1. **Type:** While choosing a Blockchain platform, one needs to define if it should be Public, Private, or Hybrid. It is just as selecting Diesel, Petrol, Electric, or Hybrid engine while buying a car.
2. **Purpose and Use Case:** Defining the purpose of the Blockchain, whether it's for tracking, financial transactions, or data security, will narrow down the options. *Selecting the key capabilities based on the IOS statement is an ideal choice.* Similarly, defining the main purpose of the car, such as daily commuting, off-roading, or long-distance travel is a crucial step.
3. **Performance and Capabilities:** Analyzing the throughput, latency, scalability, and consensus mechanisms ensures the platform's performance meets the demands of the project. It is similar to considering the car's horsepower, torque, fuel efficiency, and other performance indicators.
4. **Budget**: Different Blockchain platforms come with varying costs, including development, maintenance, and operational expenses. The choice must align with the project's budget. Cars, too, come in various price ranges, and one must balance features and quality with budget constraints.
5. **Features:** Smart contract functionality, data privacy handling, or advanced reporting tools are essential for specific use cases. While deciding a car, features like Android connect, power steering, shockers, and break type make a huge difference.
6. **Security:** Encryption, authentication mechanisms, permissions, and other such features are vital for protecting data in a Blockchain-based system. This is similar to features like airbags, anti-lock brakes, and crash test ratings in a car.
7. **Reputation**: Choosing a reputable and well-supported Blockchain platform ensures long-term stability and support. The car manufacturer's reputation for quality, reliability, and customer service can strongly influence the decision.

8. **Support:** Ongoing support, updates, community, and documentation are vital for maintaining and scaling the platform. Similarly, consideration of warranty, availability of spare parts, and servicing network ensures the car's longevity and reliability.

In conclusion, both buying a car and selecting a Blockchain platform are complex decisions that require careful consideration of various factors. The similarities highlight the intricate and multi-dimensional nature of these decisions, and in both cases, a thoughtful approach ensures alignment with needs, values, and long-term goals. Whether cruising on the highway or navigating the digital landscape, knowing what to look for makes for a smoother ride.

Other Critical Factors

1. It's essential to check which programming languages are supported to ensure compatibility and avoid integration issues.
2. Features like block explorers must be readily available for tracking blocks and transactions within the application, making the development process smoother.
3. Analysis of the Platform's Consensus Protocol with respect to the Blockchain Trilemma should be done.
4. The availability and efficiency of smart contract architecture as well as standards in a platform can help facilitate complex use cases, making this an essential criterion for selection.
5. Evaluate how well the platform can scale to meet increasing demands and handle a high volume of transactions.
6. Assess the platform's ability to interact and exchange information with other blockchain networks or existing systems within your organization (Interoperability).
7. Consider the level of community support and vendor services available for the platform.
8. Depending on the global reach of your project, you may need to consider the legal and regulatory landscape in different jurisdictions.

Vendor support is often overlooked as organizations create their internal teams. However, many Blockchain-based products have suffered or even shut down because of either less resource availability or too much dependency on a handful of resources.

As a growing concern, Energy efficiency might not be the first thing that comes to mind, but it can align with an organization's sustainability goals or public image.

Choosing the right Blockchain platform requires a thoughtful analysis that takes into account the organization's unique needs, budget considerations, and future scalability requirements.

By following the guidelines laid out above, the selection process can be more structured and aligned with the business's overarching goals.

Always consider the long-term perspective and how the platform will adapt to evolving trends and technological advancements, thus ensuring that the chosen Blockchain platform continues to provide value in the ever-changing digital landscape.

Among all these factors, the first question and the most critical one to answer is what type of Blockchain should be selected for the use case.

Therefore, let us explore the types of Blockchain categorized based on system and structure.

Types of Blockchain

Based on System

Public Blockchain

Think of a country without borders. No citizenship is needed but only a passport. Anyone can come to this country and enjoy its ecosystem. This is what a public Blockchain is like.

A public blockchain is a decentralized, open network that anyone can join and participate in. There is no need for permission to access or interact with the network. This type of blockchain offers full transparency, as all transactions are recorded on a public ledger and can be viewed by anyone.

Most popular public Blockchains are Bitcoin and Ethereum that provide a robust security measures through cryptographic functions and a consensus mechanism, where various nodes agree on the state of the blockchain.

The decentralized nature of public blockchains makes them resistant to censorship and fraud, and promotes trust among unknown participants. Since anyone can become a validator, they can also be slower and more expensive to operate due to the competitive nature of validators.

Public blockchains represent a revolutionary shift in the way that information is recorded and exchanged, democratizing financial systems and enabling innovations such as decentralized finance (DeFi).

Bitcoin and Etherum are the most prominent examples of public Blockchains.

Private Blockchain

Private Blockchain is like an exclusive country club or a gated community within a country. You need special permission to enter, and only a select few are allowed. It is controlled, secure, and only those who are members have access to its privileges. Inside this private country, the rules can be very different, customized to suit the needs of its inhabitants.

A private blockchain is a restricted network where access is controlled by a single organization or a consortium. It retains the core characteristics of blockchain technology, such as immutable record-keeping and decentralization, but does so within a confined environment.

This offers benefits in terms of efficiency, as transactions are only validated by a known set of participants, making processes quicker and less costly.

Private blockchains are often used within businesses or between trusted partners to enhance collaboration, streamline supply chain operations, or secure sensitive data. Unlike public blockchains, private blockchains offer more control over who can see and submit transactions, making them suitable for organizations that require both the transparency of a distributed ledger and the security of a restricted network.

They also allow for more customization in terms of governance and functionality to suit specific business needs.

Corda, Hyperledger, and Ethereum Enterprise are some of the prominent examples of a private blockchain.

Hybrid Blockchain

A hybrid blockchain can be likened to a special economic zone within a country that has both public areas and private sections. The public areas are open to everyone, like a beautiful national park, and represent the part of the hybrid blockchain that is transparent and accessible to all. The private sections, like exclusive resorts within the park, are only accessible to those with specific permission

Therefore, a hybrid blockchain combines the benefits of both public and private blockchains, offering a versatile solution for various use cases. Within a hybrid system, certain data might be stored on a public ledger, accessible to anyone, while other more sensitive information is kept on a private, permissioned network.

This approach can provide the transparency and integrity associated with public blockchains, while still maintaining the privacy and control inherent to private systems.

A hybrid blockchain may be used by an organization that wants to share certain data transparently with the public or specific partners while keeping other details confidential. One key advantage of a hybrid blockchain is its flexibility, allowing organizations to adapt to different regulatory, security, or business needs.

XRP(Ripple), IBM Hybrid chain, and XinFIn are some of the top Blockchain platforms enabling hybrid blockchain infrastructure.

Based on Structure

Layer 0

Layer 0 blockchain represents a foundational layer in the architecture of blockchain technology. It serves as a protocol that defines the essential elements for building a blockchain, essentially acting as the infrastructure or the groundwork upon which new blockchains can be developed.

Essentially, a Layer 0 Blockchain will have the following components:

1. Consensus protocol
2. Cryptography and hashing standards
3. Network infrastructure
4. Software development kits
5. Communication protocols

The point of defining these components is to ensure a standard modus operandi for all the future Blockchain platforms being built on top of the Layer 0 protocol.

A Layer 0 Blockchain can even allow the developer to reconfigure the size of a block. This means that the developer has the power to decide how much data can be stored in the blocks.

Therefore, while developers have access to SDKs and other customizable components, the core of all the Blockchains being built on top of the Layer 0 will always remain the same.

With this approach, the Layer 0 protocols are able to achieve more scalability, better connectivity between Blockchain protocols, and flexibility for individual solutions.

Cosmos, Avalanche (AVAX), and Polkadot are some of the prominent examples of Layer 0 technology.

Layer 1 (Blockchain Layer)

Layer 1 blockchain represents the primary layer in the architecture of blockchain technology, functioning directly on top of the Layer 0 infrastructure.

Layer 1 blockchains can be tailored to specific use cases, but they all share common elements defined at Layer 0. Basically, Layer 1 Blockchains are like Javascript libraries that developers use to build and run applications.

Components like Smart contracts, tokens, consensus algorithm, are all part of the Layer 1 Blockchain.

The purpose of these components is to facilitate a decentralized and secure environment for individual blockchain networks while adhering to the standards set by Layer 0.

With this design, the Layer 1 blockchains are capable of executing independent operations while benefiting from the scalability, connectivity, and security provided by the foundational Layer 0 protocols.

Ethereum, Bitcoin, and Binance Smart Chain are some of the prominent examples of Layer 1 technology, each providing unique functionalities and features while utilizing the underlying Layer 0 components for a cohesive and interconnected blockchain ecosystem.

Binance smart chain is built on top of the Cosmos SDK.

Layer 2 (Protocol Layer)

Layer 2 solutions can be thought of as performance-enhancing plugins or extensions that developers can integrate into their existing Layer 1 blockchain applications. These solutions might include state channels, sidechains, or Zero Knowledge Proofs like rollups, and they work in harmony with the existing infrastructure of Layer 1.

Components that are integral to Layer 1, such as Smart contracts, tokens, and consensus algorithms, can be augmented and optimized by Layer 2. This provides an additional layer of functionality, reducing transaction times, and costs, without modifying the core structure of Layer 1.

The purpose of Layer 2 is to enable faster and more efficient transactions, overcoming limitations that might be present in the Layer 1 design.

By utilizing Layer 2 solutions, developers can achieve higher throughput and responsiveness, all while maintaining the decentralized and secure nature of the original blockchain.

With this design, Layer 2 builds on the strengths of Layer 1, providing an optimized environment that enhances the user experience without compromising on the principles set by Layer 0 and implemented by Layer 1.

Examples of Layer 2 technologies include the Lightning Network for Bitcoin and the Plasma framework for Ethereum, each offering unique ways to improve transaction speeds and scalability while maintaining the underlying integrity and cohesion of the blockchain ecosystem. Arbitrium, Polygon, and Optimism are another examples of Layer 2s built for scaling Ethereum network.

These technologies act as vital additions to the existing blockchain structure, much like adding sophisticated extensions to Javascript libraries to enhance functionality and performance.

Layer 2 Blockhains are a prominent solution for solving the Blockchain Trilemma by addressing the missing property of the Blockchain.

Layer 3 (Application Layer)

Layer 3 solutions represent the application layer in the blockchain architecture, working directly with Layer 2 or even Layer 1 to bring end-user applications and interfaces to life. These solutions can be compared to the finished products built using programming frameworks or libraries, providing the final touch that allows users to interact with the underlying blockchain technology.

Components that are defined and optimized at Layer 1 and 2, such as Smart contracts, tokens, and consensus algorithms, are further refined and presented through Layer 3 in a user-friendly manner. This includes developing user interfaces, integrating third-party services, and creating customizable experiences that cater to specific use cases.

The purpose of Layer 3 is to bridge the gap between the complex underlying blockchain technology and the end users, making it accessible and usable for everyday applications. It translates the technical functionalities of Layer 1 and 2 into practical applications that users can engage with seamlessly. Much like the Social media we use without ever knowing what protocol or programming language is being used behind the scenes.

By utilizing Layer 3 solutions, developers can create diverse applications ranging from decentralized finance (DeFi) platforms to non-fungible tokens (NFTs) marketplaces, all benefiting from the scalability, security, and decentralization of the foundational layers.

With this design, Layer 3 brings the innovations of blockchain technology to the masses, transforming abstract concepts and technical procedures into tangible products and services without losing sight of the principles set by Layer 0, implemented by Layer 1, and optimized by Layer 2.

Examples of Layer 3 technologies can be found in popular decentralized applications (dApps) like Uniswap.

Layer 3 Blockchains are essential for driving adoption and usability of blockchain technology, offering tailored solutions that resonate with users while preserving the integrity and innovation of the entire blockchain architecture.

Some Comparison Points

- **User Interaction:** Layer 0 is least interactive while Layer 3 is most interactive.
- **Speed and Scalability:** Layer 1 often struggles with scalability and speed, while Layers 2 and 3 provide solutions to these issues.
- **Purpose:** Each layer serves a unique purpose, from infrastructure support at Layer 0, transaction validation at Layer 1, scalability solutions at Layer 2, to user applications at Layer 3.
- **Interdependence:** Each layer depends on the layers below it. Layer 3 applications depend on Layer 2 protocols, which in turn depend on Layer 1 blockchain, which finally depends on the Layer 0 infrastructure.
- **Visibility:** The higher layers (2 and 3) are more visible to the end-user, while the lower layers (0 and 1) work behind the scenes. A suitable order is - Layer 0 < Layer 1 < Layer 2 < Layer 3

Conclusion

If Layer 0 provides the raw materials, setting the essential guidelines for what's to come, Layer 1 builds on this foundation, acting as the engine itself, where the principles of Layer 0 are turned into a functional core that processes transactions and executes contracts. Layer 2 serves as a turbocharger, enhancing the Layer 1 engine's performance through efficiency and scalability solutions, while Layer 3 focuses on user experience and interface.

Blockchain Decision Models

Selecting the right Blockchain platform is the next big decision, after defining the need for Blockchain.

To define if or why a particular solution needs Blockchain, there are several methods commonly known as decision models. Each model brings unique insights to the table, assisting in making informed decisions about whether to integrate a blockchain solution and what type might be most suitable for a given scenario.

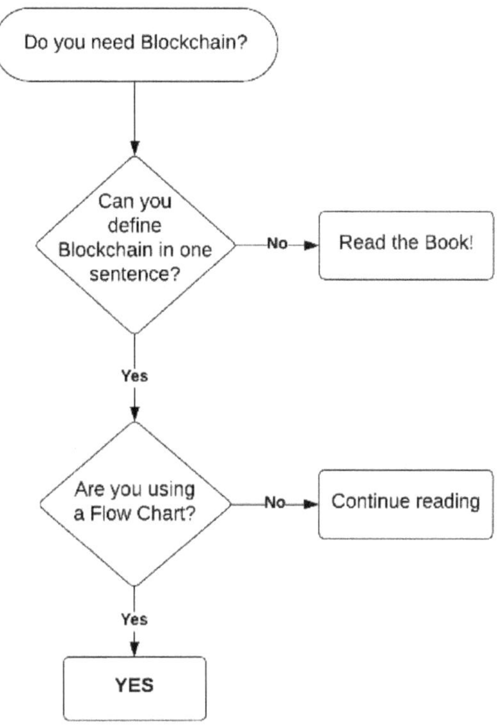

1. D. Birch Model: Need vs. Solution

The D. Birch Model emphasizes on the identification of real-world problems. Instead of focusing solely on the technology, this model urges a consideration of the actual challenges at hand. It suggests that a blockchain might not be the initial requirement, but rather a potential solution once the underlying problems are clearly defined. By addressing the root issues, organizations can determine if implementing a blockchain is a strategic move to resolve those problems.

Focus: Blockchain as a solution, not a need. Emphasizes on addressing existing problems that might eventually lead to a blockchain application.

2. Birch-Brown-Parulava Model: Permissionless vs. Permissioned Ledgers

The Birch-Brown-Parulava Model is suitable for making a choice between permissionless and permissioned ledgers. It aids decision-makers in understanding the intricacies of these ledger types in context of distributed systems. The model brings attention to the possibility of public networks maintained by select validators, which challenges the conventional perception of public networks as open to all. By delving into these distinctions, organizations can make informed choices between permissionless and permissioned ledgers.

Focus: Distributed ledger concept. Helps differentiate between permissionless and permissioned ledgers.

3. B. Suichies Model: Public vs. Private Blockchains

The B. Suichies Model places its focus on delineating between public and private blockchain implementations. It introduces the notion that intra-firm blockchains, designed to operate within a single organization, might not adequately address underlying issues. This model prompts organizations to reflect on whether their existing problems are systemic, possibly requiring broader solutions than an internal blockchain can provide.

Focus: Differences between public and private blockchains. Suggests that intra-firm blockchains might not solve fundamental issues.

4. IBM Model: Privacy and Alternatives

The IBM Model introduces a market-oriented perspective and addresses privacy concerns. It encourages decision-makers to go beyond smart contracts and consider the inherent properties of Blockchain. Furthermore, it raises a pivotal question: whether data sharing or data privacy is of higher priority. By focusing on these dynamics, organizations can assess the appropriateness of a blockchain solution, understanding their data-centric needs and whether a blockchain aligns with their privacy requirements

Focus: Advocates a "market" approach. Encourages exploring alternative approach other than smart contracts. Raises the question of data sharing vs. privacy.

5. Cathy Mulligan Model: Blockchain or not

Cathy Mulligan's model underlines the importance of carefully assessing the actual challenges, benefits, collaboration dynamics, and trust issues before deciding to implement blockchain technology. By addressing these questions, organizations can make informed choices and avoid adopting blockchain as a buzzword-driven solution, focusing instead on its true potential to bring value and innovation to their operations.

Focus: Argues the need for Blockchain. Emphasizes relevant questions, particularly distrust among contributors. Suggests "can't do efficiently" and "further research needed" point towards not using blockchain.

For someone who is starting their Blockchain journey, Cathy Mulligan model is the most appropriate one. The flow chart of this model can be found on the next page.

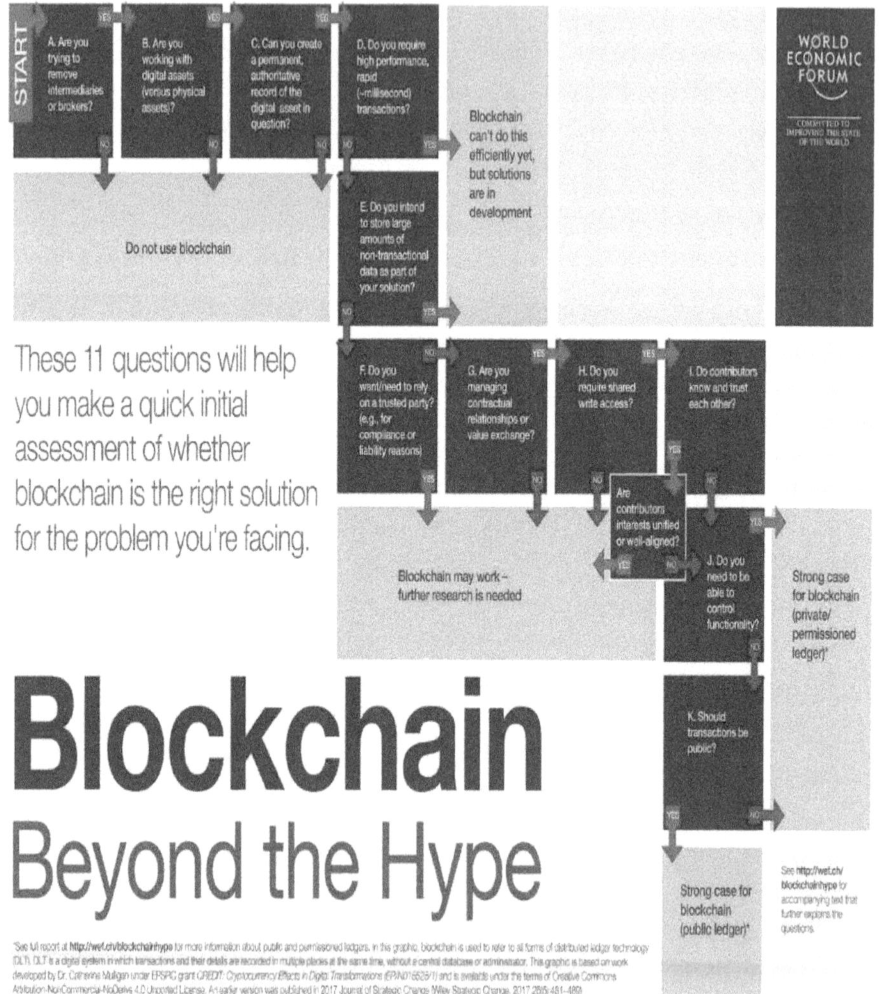
START
A. Are you trying to remove intermediaries or brokers?
B. Are you working with digital assets (versus physical assets)?
C. Can you create a permanent, authoritative record of the digital asset in question?
D. Do you require high performance, rapid (~millisecond) transactions?
Blockchain can't do this efficiently yet, but solutions are in development
WORLD ECONOMIC FORUM
Do not use blockchain
E. Do you intend to store large amounts of non-transactional data as part of your solution?
These 11 questions will help you make a quick initial assessment of whether blockchain is the right solution for the problem you're facing.
F. Do you want/need to rely on a trusted party? (e.g., for compliance or liability reasons)
G. Are you managing contractual relationships or value exchange?
H. Do you require shared write access?
I. Do contributors know and trust each other?
Are contributors interests unified or well-aligned?
Blockchain may work – further research is needed
J. Do you need to be able to control functionality?
Strong case for blockchain (private/ permissioned ledger)*
K. Should transactions be public?
Blockchain
Beyond the Hype
Strong case for blockchain (public ledger)*
See http://wef.ch/ blockchainhype for accompanying text that further explores the questions.
YES
NO

Bonus Chapter

CAREERS IN BLOCKCHAIN

It is a common belief that Blockchain is highly technical since it involves complex concepts such as Consensus algorithms and Hashing.

Here is a question that brings a new perspective to this belief.

The Internet is a complex network that relies on a variety of technologies and protocols to function such as TCP, HTTP, VPN, Firewall, DNS, and many more.

If a person does not know any of the components of the Internet, will they be able to work in the digital space?

The answer is YES. When it comes to building a career in any industry, core knowledge of the industry is always a plus but it is never the only way to build a career.

Take Basketball for example, there are players who know how to play but there are commentators, critics, food vendors in the stadium, people who build the stadium, channels that stream the game, advertisers, agents who handle those advertisers, shoe manufacturers, and so many more people involved.

In a similar way, building a career in Blockchain is subjective to the interests and skills of a person rather than the technology itself.

Here are a few careers that have gained traction over the past few years in Blockchain:

- **Blockchain Sales Manager:** Drives sales efforts for blockchain products and services, identifying prospects, and closing deals to achieve revenue goals.
- **Blockchain Business Development Executive:** Identifies growth opportunities, builds strategic partnerships, and expands the market reach of blockchain-related products and services.

- **Blockchain Content Creator:** Specializes in creating engaging content like articles, blogs, and videos to educate and promote awareness of blockchain concepts and projects.
- **Blockchain Marketing Specialist:** Plans and executes marketing strategies, including SEO, social media, and email marketing, to promote and increase visibility of blockchain brands and products.
- **Community manager:** Focuses on building and maintaining relationships with various community stakeholders, organizing events, and fostering a strong community around a blockchain project.
- **Blockchain UX/UI Designer:** Designs user-friendly interfaces for decentralized applications, ensuring an engaging and intuitive user experience.
- **Blockchain Security Specialist:** Focuses on securing blockchain systems, identifying vulnerabilities, and protecting against potential attacks and breaches.
- **Blockchain Developer:** Designs and implements blockchain protocols, smart contracts, and architecture, providing the backbone for decentralized applications.
- **Smart Contract Engineer:** Specializes in writing, testing, and implementing smart contracts on blockchain platforms, enabling automated, trustless transactions.
- **Blockchain Project Manager:** Coordinates and oversees blockchain projects, ensuring alignment with goals, timelines, and resources, bridging the technical and business sides.
- **Blockchain Legal Consultant:** Provides legal advice on regulatory, compliance, and intellectual property law pertaining to blockchain and cryptocurrency activities.

ABOUT THE AUTHOR

Harman is a pioneering influencer in the Blockchain and Web3 domain, with a career that reflects a rich tapestry of experience and innovation. Beginning his career as a developer, he interfaced with esteemed financial teams as a consultant, eventually paving the way to ambassadorial roles for multimillion-dollar companies. Organiser of Punjab's significant Web3 summit under Panjab DAO, he has actively contributed to India's thriving Web3 ecosystem.

A passionate educator, Harman has mentored over 10,000 students and faculty across prestigious institutions in the form of Faculty development programs, Seminars, and Workshops, earning recognition such as the Amity Excellence Award. As a prolific writer, with 2,000+ blogs and 8 whitepapers to his credit, his insights have benefited industry giants in the Blockchain space.

www.ingramcontent.com/pod-product-compliance
Ingram Content Group UK Ltd.
Pitfield, Milton Keynes, MK11 3LW, UK
UKHW062258290726
14090UKWH00017B/761

9 798890 679932